YOUR GUIDE TO CORPORATE SURVIVAL

BY

SCOTT CHOATE

Illustrated by PAUL MICHAEL DAVIES

CCC PUBLICATIONS • LOS ANGELES

Published by

CCC Publications
20306 Tau Place
Chatsworth, CA 91311

Manufactured in the United States of America

Cover art by Paul Michael Davies

Cover color by Suzanne Carroll Feinsinger

Cover production by The Creative Place

ISBN: 0-918259-20-7

If your local U.S. bookstore is out of stock, copies of this book may be obtained by mailing check or money order for $4.95 per book (plus $1.50 to cover sales tax, postage and handling) to: CCC Publications; 20306 Tau Place; Chatsworth, CA 91311.

First Printing—9/89

DEDICATION

This book is dedicated to my wife Nancy, who helped turn my writing from a hobby into a profession. She did everything for this book but write it, including editing, marketing and putting up with a writer's idiosyncracies. She contributed valuable ideas, comments, constructive criticism and inestimable support. Without her, this book would still be sitting in the word processor instead of in your hands.

ACKNOWLEDGEMENTS

I would like to give thanks to the many people whose support was integral to this book.

To Betty and David, who taught me to speak my own mind no matter what anybody else thought. To Elaine, George, Marty, Maya and all my relatives and friends who understood when writing allowed me little time to spend with them. To Kay King, for nurturing my creativity. To Alexander Choate and Albert Lane, for the inspiration their idealism provides, as well as their early enthusiasm for this book. To Eileen Koprowski, Mark Nordman, Jeannie Peurasaari and Susan Young for their crucial efforts on the book's behalf. To Mark Chutick and Cliff Carle for their immediate, overwhelming and never-wavering support. One couldn't hope for a more dedicated publisher and editor. To Paul Michael Davies, whose illustrations made a significant contribution to the book.

To you, the reader, for accepting "he" and "she" as they are used herein. My use of gender should not be taken as definitive, as it is a product of my own upbringing, background and experiences. Yes, Virginia, there can be male secretaries and female chairpersons of the board.

Finally ... to the many people I've met in corporations whose complaints go unheard and dreams of getting out are as yet unfulfilled...

THIS BOOK IS FOR YOU!

AUTHOR'S FORWARD:

Corporate Philosophy

There is only one corporate philosophy:

MAKE MONEY!

Nothing else matters to a corporation.

Not efficiency. Not making a better product or providing a better service. ***Not even you.***

Don't be misled by public relations slogans like "quality comes first", "service before profit", "our employees are family", etc. These are only smoke screens concocted by very creative public relations professionals to disguise the true *raison d'etre* of corporations:

To make MEGA-BUCKS!

Don't ever forget this.

EVER.

IT'S NOT JUST A CORPORATE PHILOSOPHY, HARRIS — IT'S POETRY, SHEER POETRY!

TABLE OF CONTENTS

Part Three: Corporate Politics

Part Four: Unlocking Corporate Secrets

Part Five:
Taking Advantage of Your Corporation

Part Six:
Getting Out of A Corporation

INTRODUCTION

cor-po-ra-tion (kor' per a' shun) n. 1. A legal entity that one group of people (shareholders and corporate management) forms for the sole purpose of screwing the ever-loving crap out of another group of people (employees and customers).

Like it or not, we are living in the ***age of the corporation.***

Within ten years, corporations will probably have their own flags. Within twenty years, government will probably give up being the middle man and instruct us to pay our taxes directly to corporations. Within thirty years, corporations will finally stop feigning subservience to governments and take what they consider to be their rightful place in the world ... as actual nations. Your children will probably find themselves living in Houston, Exxon ... or Paris, Renault ... or Osaka, Sony.

But we're getting a little ahead of ourselves.

In 1886, the United States Supreme Court decided that corporations are, for legal purposes, "persons" (Santa Clara County vs. Southern Pacific Railroad). This decision gave corporations legal protections that only human beings had had before. But instead of becoming more human, corporations went the other way. They used this case as justification to treat others with all the tenderness and sensitivity of a rapist.

Since that case, mankind has been cursed (or blessed, depending upon your point of view or annual income) with the increasing dominance of corporations in every aspect of our lives.

If you work for a corporation, you spend approximately 2,000 hours there a year. This leaves approximately 2,900 hours for sleeping, and approximately 3,860 hours for whatever else it is you enjoy doing. Most people use these 3,860 hours for eating, making love, mowing the lawn, shopping, watching television, etc. Of course, many people spend quite a few of these 3,860 hours worrying about what will go wrong during the 2,000 hours they spend at work. Or worse, worrying about what new horrors corporate executives are preparing — or who's scheming to get them fired.

But that isn't all!

Corporate tentacles reach into our lives in other ways, too. Medical and dental benefits, life insurance, perks ranging from discounts on company products to company cars, free stationery items for those bold enough to walk out with them ... all of these things are more and more making the corporation an integral part of our lives.

What's so bad about that, you ask. You work for a corporation, it pays you and gives you some benefits, and all you have to invest is 2,000 hours a year and a little worry.

If this is so wonderful, then why are you so unhappy? Why do you dread the alarm clock each morning for fear of what's lurking behind your office door today? Why is "job security" something you've never felt?

Why is a book about learning to survive working in a corporation even necessary? It seems natural to worry about surviving an automobile accident, but why do so many of us worry about surviving our ***jobs***?

The key to survival is understanding the dark truth about what ***really*** goes on inside corporations.

In this book, we will pierce the corporate shield which protects these and other secrets corporations don't want you to uncover. We will explore what corporations say, and what they actually do. We will dissect much of what you will encounter from your first day on the job until your last. We will answer such questions as:

1. What perks, benefits and freebies can I hope to con the corporation out of?

2. During the job interview, how much can I exaggerate about myself and get away with?

3. What are the chances of successful sexual pursuits on the job?

4. How do I deal with all the various personalities — corporate "red tape", corporate backstabbing and b.s. — and still come out ***on top***?

5. How can I prevent getting fired ... or get even in the event that I do?

6. How can I play the ***game*** of corporate politics and ***win***?

These and many more questions, essential to your survival in a corporation, will be answered in the pages that follow.

In short, we will discover ***practical*** and ***meaningful*** ways to survive working in a corporation. We will also learn to give corporations a dose of their own medicine!

If you'd like to learn how to do this with the ease and confidence of a professional, read on ...

PART ONE

GETTING INTO

A CORPORATION

INTRODUCTION

Getting Into A Corporation

Considering the number of corporations in the world today, you'd think getting into one of them shouldn't be all that difficult. At least not for reasonably intelligent, hard working people who can dress themselves and eat with utensils.

Wrong!

These qualities are no longer sufficient. Not when so many people are out of work that corporations can pick and choose from an ample inventory of labor. So, if being one of the best and brightest won't get you a job in this day and age, what will?

Kissing ass!

Today you must give complete submission to the corporate world.

There is only one circumstance left under which you can withhold submission ... if you are ***independently wealthy***. (If you ***are*** independently wealthy, you have no reason to work for a corporation unless you own it.)

If you're not in this small and select group, pucker up and ***start kissing!***

WELL, HARRIS? WE'RE WAITING...

CHAPTER I

The Job Search

The methods of finding a job haven't changed much over the years. Neither has prostitution, and the two activities have definite similarities.

You get yourself noticed any way you can, impress whomever has the power to hire you, and don't make too many outrageous demands.

To do this, there are some basic tools you will need, and rituals you will have to endure. The most basic tool is...

Your Resumé

The first thing you'll need when trying to find a job in a corporation is a resumé.

Volumes have been written about how to compile them. Some crooks even charge outrageous sums of money to do it for you. If you haven't mastered the technical aspects of resumé writing, buy one of these books or pay one of the crooks. But no matter what they tell you ...

DON'T BE AFRAID TO STRETCH THE TRUTH!

A little exaggeration never hurt anyone! No employer has the time to check each and every detail of all the resumés they receive. So, if your resumé doesn't look good enough, beef it up a little. We're not talking perjury ... just enough creative writing to make yourself as marketable as possible. Huge lies will eventually get you into trouble.

For example, if your last position was Mail Clerk, don't put Vice President, Mail Operations on your resumé. Mail Coordinator, however, is a title you can probably get away with.

The "Educational Background" section of your resumé is another good place to exercise creativity. Nobody is going to call your university and find out if you really graduated Magna Cum Laude or were President of the High I.Q. Club.

Don't listen to those purists who say that a resumé should be as accurate as a legal document ... every job title exact, dates precise, every responsibility listed without embellishment. These people live in constant fear that a prospective employer will commission an F.B.I. background check on them — that if ***any*** discrepancy is found, they'll be sentenced to 15-20 at Leavenworth.

People who think this way make excellent employees. But guess what? They already have jobs, and probably weren't so high and mighty about accuracy before they got them. So...

HAVE NO FEAR! LET YOUR IMAGINATION FLOW!

You should also be aware of and obey what are called ***THE DON'TS OF RESUMÉ WRITING***. These are simple rules designed to keep things out of your resumé that turn prospective employers off. Here are some of the more important ***don'ts***...

Don't try to be cute when writing your resumé. Listing hobbies like raising bunnies or painting mermaids on the sides of vans isn't going to speed up the employment process. If you feel the need to include off-hours activities, make them job-related. Corporations love to hear that you spend your nights and weekends doing things that feel like work. Professional organizations are great to list. If you don't belong to one, make one up. For example, if you are a computer programmer, include your membership in the "American Computer Programmers Professional Management Organization". You don't need to mention that this is an informal group of you and your friends who get drunk on Saturday nights and try to hack your way into the Pentagon's mainframe computer.

Don't list people as references unless you are certain that they will compare you favorably with the Pope. If nothing else, prospective employers ***do*** check references. Many people make the mistake of listing former bosses whom they don't know personally. Sometimes these bosses are unreliable, and give honest assessments of your work, including "areas of needed improvement". If you want something negative said about you, why don't you just call up your prospective employer and tell him you're not qualified? You'll accomplish the same end.

If the best reference you can come up with is a disgruntled bill collector, enlist a friend to help you. Nobody would ever guess that it is your best friend who answers his phone,"Vice President, Personnel", then gives such a glowing portrait of your work performance that it brings tears to the eyes of hardened dockworkers.

And finally, ***don't*** ever allow a gap between the ending date of one job and the starting date of the next. Budding young personnel recruiters are taught to look for unexplained intervals between jobs, because these are sometimes clues to uncovering unacceptable corporate behavior in a prospective employee's background (i.e. suing a company for wrongful termination, being fired for cause, or serving time in prison). Unless you were kidnapped, held hostage in Beirut and it was all over the news, try not to show inexplicable gaps between jobs. Women, remember that pregnancy is no longer an excuse in the corporate world for not working. Many corporations feel that giving the afternoon off for childbirth is plenty.

If you do have any kind of a gap in employment that you'd rather a prospective employer not know about, fill it in with something that sounds legitimate. "Consulting" is usually the best bet. Consulting is vague and virtually untraceable. You can always say that your client was the government, that your work was top secret, that anybody who asks you more than this about it is obviously not a 100% pure red-blooded American.

No matter what you put in your resumé, it could very well be the first view a prospective employer has of you.

If it doesn't get his attention, ***you*** won't have a chance to. So, don't be afraid to make your resumé look as good as you can, using whatever means you must short of clipping a $100 bill to it.

If your resumé looks good, you'll already have one foot in the door when they call you in for...

IT'S FROM MY BOSS. IT SAYS,
"CONGRATULATIONS ON THIS HAPPY OCCASION — SEE YOU BRIGHT AND EARLY MONDAY MORNING."

The Interview

Once your resumé lands on the right desk, your long trek through the minefield into a corporation will begin. Odds are, your first interview will be with a Human Resources (Personnel) recruiter.

For this interview, you must be prepared to convince the recruiter that there is nothing else in the world you'd rather do than the job for which you are applying. If you need to stretch the truth a bit, go ahead! Recruiters only want to make sure you're reasonably qualified for the job, and that you aren't an ax murderer. They usually have only a passing knowledge of what you should be able to do.

Above all, do ***NOT*** say what comes naturally. Recruiters have a tendency to ask questions they learned in college. These questions are ridiculous, and deserve sarcastic answers. Unfortunately, sarcastic answers will not get you a job in a corporation.

Below is a helpful chart which lists typical interview questions, natural responses (replies you would ***love*** to give), and the ***correct*** (in order to get the job) response:

Recruiter: "Let me throw a hypothetical question at you. You discover an employee drinking on the job. What do you do?"

Natural Response: "Let him drink. Who the hell cares?! He'll probably make better decisions drunk than most people around here do sober."

Correct Response: "Report the incident to Human Resources immediately!"

Recruiter: "Let me throw another hypothetical question at you. You discover a fellow employee has been embezzling thousands of dollars from the company. What do you do?"

Natural Response: "Figure out how he's doing it, triple the amount and do it myself. If I tried to feed my family on the salary you're offering, we'd be better off begging in the streets of Calcutta."

Correct Response: "Report the incident to Human Resources immediately!"

Recruiter: "Let me throw still another hypothetical question at you..."

Natural Response: "Enough of these stupid hypothetical questions already! You obviously learned about life from a textbook."

Correct Response: "Great! I love hypothetical questions! Especially intellectually stimulating ones like the kind you're asking."

After you pass muster with the recruiter, your next stop will be an interview with your prospective boss. You won't be able to ***b.s.*** in this interview, because your boss presumably knows something about the job he or she is hiring you for.

In this age where more and more people don't have any guts, and thus make fewer and fewer decisions, you may have to interview with your boss' boss or your boss' boss' boss. This is because no one wants to take the responsibility if you turn out to be ***THE WRONG PERSON***. If that happens, everyone involved wants to be able to blame your hiring on someone else.

As you will learn, once you've worked in a corporation for a while, ***passing the corporate buck*** is one of the most important keys to corporate survival.

The thing that most interviewees do not realize is that the people doing the interviewing are probably saying to themselves, "I've got more important things to do than this." They want you to be "the one" so they can get back to whatever they think is more important.

At all times, whether you are writing your resumé or selling yourself in an interview, act like you are "the one". Your chances of getting the job will increase markedly.

Those who don't act like they were created especially for the job usually don't get it. People like this are one of the reasons why dictionaries contain the word "loser".

...AGAIN, HYPOTHETICALLY SPEAKING, WHAT WOULD YOUR RESPONSE BE IF A HUMAN RESOURCES RECRUITER WERE TO GIVE YOU A JOB ON THE CONDITION THAT YOU KICK BACK 20 BUCKS A WEEK TO HIM PERSONALLY?

CHAPTER II

The Job Offer

Once you've kissed enough corporate butt to convince the right people you're the gift from Heaven they've been searching for, you will be made a job offer.

By the time a corporation does this, it is ***in*** pretty deep. Several people have interviewed you, others have approved of your hiring, references have been checked, etc. This is a lot of work that would have to be repeated should you turn them down. They ***want*** you to accept their offer.

This is your last chance to get any meaningful concessions from them. Once you accept, you have no more bargaining power.

So, don't be shy. Ask for more money, longer vacations, better benefits, a more important title, a bigger office ... ***anything and everything you possibly can!***

Money, Benefits & Perks

Without exception, the most important part of a job offer is ***money!***

Benefits and perks are nice, and sometimes help fluff up a mediocre offer, but you can't pay the rent or buy groceries with dental insurance.

The money that comes home with you each week in your paycheck is the only thing that really counts. And yet, you'd be surprised how many people don't negotiate this figure. They are so grateful that a corporation is actually offering them money to do something, they take it like a starving man who's just been offered a filet mignon.

In most cases, a ***petite*** filet mignon.

You need to remember that, even though they say their offer is final, corporations are ***always*** prepared to negotiate. Put them on the spot!

But there's one thing you must never do:

NEVER, NEVER, NEVER respond directly to questions like, ***"What is your desired salary range?"*** or ***"How much are you currently making?"*** Instead, ask them to make you an offer. Tell them that your salary must be based on your new job responsibilities, not what you made at your old job.

The reason for this is simple. Unless you ask for some outrageous figure they reserve only for top executives, you'll lock yourself into a salary level you're going to be stuck with much longer than you think. Granted, you'll be eligible for increases, but these increases will be based on a percentage of your current salary. So, if you accept a job for $30,000, don't expect a raise to $60,000, or $50,000, or even $40,000. The only way you're going to receive a raise like that is to get a really ***big*** promotion.

Don't hold your breath.

Unfortunately, sometimes there is no way to get around telling them how much you want. In this case, always ask for ***more***.

In today's economic jungle, corporations must continually prove their economic manhood. Whatever something costs, they have to pay less or risk loss of face. They will chop your figure down, even if it is already low to begin with.

To get around this, come up with the figure you want and add 20%. The corporation will immediately chop off 20% just to show you who's boss.

In the end, you'll still get what you want, which is what truly counts.

Benefits and perks should be given importance during job negotiations ***after*** you've settled on a salary. Many times there will seemingly be no give and take on these points because corporations set standards for different levels of employees.

Ignore the standards. Ask for more. Just be creative about it. Whenever they deny one of your requests, ask for something else.

For example, if they tell you that you will be entitled to one week of vacation during the first year of employment, ask for more sick leave. If they tell you the corporation doesn't offer company cars at your level, ask for stock options. If they tell you the company doesn't offer stock options, ask for an automobile allowance.

You may or may not get more money, benefits or perks, but you'll never know without asking. You'll also never get them after you accept a job offer, so go for them ***now!***

I'LL SEE YOUR $30K PLUS FULL DENTAL,
AND RAISE YOU $10K WITH A COMPANY CAR...

Title

Although not as important as money, your title should not be passed over lightly.

Titles are, of course, worthless. But then so are small pieces of green paper with serial numbers and pictures of presidents on them. It's the value we place on these little pieces of paper called "bucks" that makes them worth something.

So, too, with titles!

Your title will determine not only your authority, but how people interact with and treat you in your new job. If you are a clerk, they will treat you like a clerk. If you are a vice president, they will treat you like one. If you are a vice president who acts like a clerk, they will treat you like a jerk.

In today's corporate universe, titles are multiplying as fast as cancer-causing agents. When negotiating with a prospective employer over what you will be called, it will be helpful to refer to the **GENERIC TITLE CHART** on the next page. This chart explains what titles really mean, no matter what your specialization is.

GENERIC TITLE CHART

TITLE	WHAT IT REALLY MEANS
Clerk	The lowest form of intelligent corporate life. A title to be avoided at all costs. Anyone who proudly admits to being a clerk should get comfortable with the title. They're going to have it for a ***long*** time.
Coordinator, Supervisor, Manager, Director, etc.	All of these titles mean the same thing. They form that vast corporate wasteland called "middle management". This is where the work either gets done or a massive bureaucracy festers. If you end up with one of these titles, move up and out of it as soon as you can. Otherwise, it will stick to you like a leech.
Vice President	The most overused title in corporations. V.P. stripes are given to employees when they've gone as far as they're going to go in a corporation and there's nothing left to give them in the way of salary increases, promotions, bigger offices, etc.
Senior and Executive Vice Presidents	Variations on the V.P. theme and just as overused. Often used just to give V.P.'s someone to report to.
President, Chairman, Chief Executive Officer	If there is only one of these in a corporation, then the title means something. If all of these (or more) are present, get ready for a bloodbath!

No matter what job you're trying to get, always go for the highest title you can. Try to make it better than your current one. The last thing you want is for your resumé to look like a saga of lateral moves.

If you can't get the title you want, ask for some variation of the one they're offering. Even the most mundane of titles can be made to sound important. For example, if they're offering you ***Director of Finance***, go for ***Executive Director, Corporate Finance***. It may not mean anything more important, but it sure sounds good!

Whatever your title, don't be misled into thinking that a good title will solve all your problems. Ninety percent of your success (or failure) will be directly attributable to the way you carry yourself. Always act like you should be one level above where you are.

If you act any other way, you might as well take your place next to the doormat for people to wipe their shoes on.

Your Office

It cannot be stressed too strongly how important your office is, whether it's a traditional office with four walls, an open-air cubicle or simply a desk. Your office should be the most important thing to you after salary.

For men, it is just as important as penis size. ***Big*** is better! For women, it is just as important as breast size. Office size differs from penis and breast size only in that there is a limit to how big a penis or breasts can be and still be manageable. There is ***no*** limit to how big people want their offices to be, because in a corporation, ***office size equals power***. The person who tells you he doesn't care about the size of his office is a loser. Do not look for his name to appear on the front page of the Wall Street Journal.

In addition to size, several other factors are important in determining how your office ranks. Some examples follow. You should demand as many of these as you can get away with...

OFFICE CRITERIA	IMPORTANCE
1. Window	***One*** used to be a hot ticket item. Now, if you don't have a corner office with at least 10 windows, you're a clerk.
2. New Furniture	Only worth bonus points if it costs the company more than $30,000. If it comes "from storage", you're a clerk.
3. Incandescent Lighting (Spots)	Anything less won't do. The only people who have fluorescent lighting are ... you guessed it ... clerks!
4. Floor Level	Just as important now as it was fifty years ago. The higher you are in the building, the higher you are in the corporation.
5. Remote Control Door Closer Button	Fastest growing status item. Used to be for executives too lazy to get up to close their office doors. Now used to slam the door in people's faces by remote control ... ***the ultimate insult!***

After you accept a job offer and begin working for a corporation, treat your office like your first-born. If you are ever told by the musclebrains who control such things that you must move to a new office, don't go until you are assured that your new office is better than your present one. Chain yourself to your desk, nail your furniture to the floor, hire armed thugs to keep the movers out ... anything to protect your territory. If you must go, insist upon an office with at least one more square foot, one more window, or one floor up. Appearance counts just as much as substance in corporations, and you must ***always*** give the appearance of moving ***up***.

The person who allows him or herself to be moved from a 500 square foot corner office on the 45th floor to a windowless cubicle in the basement better get used to going down. That's the only direction they're ever going to know.

On the other hand, do not become so engrossed in the intricacies of office politics that they become more important than your job. You will quickly lose your colleagues' respect if you are perceived as one whose interest in the color of his couch is more important than his job responsibilities.

Don't let this happen to you.

The way to avoid it is to be subtle about your office requests, especially when negotiating a job offer. Never say things like, "I deserve a large office because I'm important." A better way of putting it is, "I'll need a large office because of all the meetings I take with large groups of people."

It's a boldface lie, of course, but it will do the trick without damaging your reputation.

After you get the best offer you can out of a corporation ... when you don't think you can push them any further on salary, title, benefits, perks, office demands, etc., ***always*** tell them you need a day or two to think it over. Even if they are offering you the dream package of a lifetime. Corporations must never get the impression you are so eager to work for them that you'll take anything they offer on the spot.

If you reduce yourself to that, you might as well put the leg irons on yourself and throw away the key. Once you sign on the dotted line, the torture begins...

LOOKS LIKE BARSTOW IS ON A FAST TRACK HERE — THEY'RE MOVING HIS OFFICE TO THE ROOF...

CHAPTER III

The First Day

After you accept a job offer, anticipation and nervousness about your new job will grow until ...

The first day!

Everyone who gets through the dreaded ***first day*** with their sanity intact invariably compares it to a combination of:

a. Quitting smoking.

b. Getting mugged.

c. Jumping into a pool and forgetting how to swim.

No words ... no amount of careful planning can completely prepare you for the ***first day***.

The First People You'll Meet

This is the day when everybody who comes into contact with you evaluates everything about you ... your looks, your intelligence, your experience ... and then gathers just out of hearing range to talk about you. This is the day when you feel as if you know absolutely nothing about what you've been hired to do, that you're trapped in a nightmare with no escape. This is the day when your boss finds out whether he's hired his savior ... or made the worst mistake of his professional career.

Don't despair. There is a way to get through the first day. One simple trick is to be prepared for the different personalities you'll meet. Although there are many waiting in the wings, the three most common types that usually come out of the woodwork on the first day are:

1. The ***"Mother Teresa"***. In one word, the Mother Teresa type is ... nice. She is also a nearly extinct animal on the corporate landscape. This is because corporate pressure to make money at any cost doesn't leave people much time to be considerate to their fellow employees.

Mother Teresa is happy to see you because she knows how much the company needs you. She goes out of her way to introduce you to the corporation ... its people, its procedures, its pitfalls.

Mother Teresa is your friend. She shows you where the supply closet is, voluntarily sits next to you in the employee lounge, even shows you how to use the fax machine. Most other people don't remember what it was like on their first day ... that a new employee has such elementary needs, but Mother Teresa does.

If the truth be known, there is a little larceny in Mother Teresa's heart ... your arrival probably benefits her in one way or another. Still, having someone nice to turn to is better than ...

2. The ***"Back Stabber"***. The Back Stabber is becoming more and more prevalent because of the increasingly cutthroat nature of corporate life. The Back Stabber will do anything to hold onto his job. Any new employee is automatically considered a threat until he or she can be tamed.

The Back Stabber will go out of his way to make your first day (and all that follow) as difficult as possible. He will purposely withhold information vital to your job performance, letting you make mistakes he could prevent so that he can say, "The new person doesn't seem to be working out."

Be especially vigilant for Back Stabbers who masquerade as Mother Teresas. They pretend to show you the ropes, but only the ones that will hang you. For example, this type of two-faced corporate snake might advise you to close down the Atlanta office because it isn't profitable — all the while knowing that the Chairman frequently visits the Atlanta office because his mistress works there.

3. ***"The Corporate Lifer"***. While Mother Teresas and Backstabbers come at you from every direction on your first day, Corporate Lifers are not so bold. Yet they are there, peeking at you from behind ficus trees and water fountains. You can't miss them.

The Corporate Lifer is stuck. He's worked for corporations (sometimes just one, and in only one capacity) his entire life. He'll probably die there. Just like his counterpart in prison, he knows nothing but what he's learned within the four walls surrounding him. Consequently, he has a dim view of newcomers. They represent change to his way of thinking, his policies, his procedures. ***"...because we've always done it this way"*** is his favorite answer to every question.

Newcomers also represent the possibility that they were sent to replace Corporate Lifers. Consequently, Lifers burrow deep inside corporations and settle in offices and cubicles where people of consequence rarely venture. When they do, Lifers take on a chameleonic aura, and become as much a part of the office as a desk or a chair.

The Lifer can be just as much of an obstacle as the Back Stabber. He's just more subtle. He doesn't attack you ... he just doesn't ***help*** you.

So, how do you deal with these people?

LIFERS, KNIFERS AND SAINTS

Mother Teresa is easy ... take advantage of her! Take her to lunch. Learn as much as you can from her. Help her with anything she asks for, even if you find yourself doing her job. You need all the friends you can get on the first day, and there's no reason to spurn the friendship of the one person who offers it to you. Plus, you can build a network of supporters by starting with Mother Teresa and working outward. If you ever expect to accomplish anything in a corporation (including holding onto your job), you will need as many supporters as you can find.

The Back Stabber must be taught the limits of his transgressions. Be nice, but don't hesitate to point out each and every time the Back Stabber is wrong. Drop hints about how the Back Stabber's areas of responsibility are "out of control". Publicly suggest ways for him to improve the productivity of his department. Tell everybody how much you respect his years of service to the company, but now it's time for younger, more professional people to take over. Give him as much "consideration" as he is giving you!

If you come across a Lifer, how you act depends upon the circumstances. If the Lifer reports to you, threaten to fire him just for the hell of it. You don't need a reason, and it is better if you don't have one. This will scare the Lifer into either productivity or retirement. If the Lifer doesn't report to you, leave him alone. He'll eventually draw the fire of some ambitious cost cutter.

Better him than you!

If you don't master the techniques of dealing with these people, you'll never have the chance to do your job. If you don't do your job, obviously you won't have it for long. So, learn to get along.

And, if you think the pitfalls these people set for you are hazardous, wait 'til you see the ***big trap*** the corporation has lying in wait for you...

The Code of Ethics

One of the most objectionable things you'll be instructed to do on your first day in a corporation is to sign your company's Code of Ethics.

Most people think loyalty oaths went out of style in the 1950's ... the days when a person had to swear allegiance to their country right or wrong, disavow any radical leanings, turn in friends.

You may not have to take a loyalty oath to your country any longer (unless you work for the government or the defense industry) — but you do have to take a loyalty oath to your corporation.

This oath is called the Code of Ethics.

Your signature on their Code of Ethics allows the corporation to use you as a scapegoat for anything that goes wrong. Typical Codes of Ethics provide that, should an employee break even any minor stipulation of the Code, the corporation is free to fire, sue or do whatever it wants to the employee.

This means that if you knowingly or unknowingly commit any misdeed or illegality, no matter how common a practice it is, no matter how much you were encouraged to do so by your boss either through direct or implied orders, the corporation can heap all the blame on you and step aside. After all, YOU signed the Code of Ethics.

Good deal for the corporation. As usual ... bad deal for the employee.

Unfortunately, there is no way to avoid signing the Code of Ethics. Who in their right mind would object to associating themselves with **ETHICS**?! Only the kind of ingrate who doesn't **REALLY** deserve the job he's just gotten.

You can, however, question the ethics of your corporation. Has it set forth its own statement of ethics, signed by the majority shareholders and senior management? Has it forsworn the types of unethical conduct which have become commonplace in today's corporations?

For example, if you work for a construction company, what is its policy about digging foundations for buildings? If its construction crews come across a historical site ... say an old cemetery, do they stop digging? Or have they been instructed to "mistake" headstones for "old rocks" and just bulldoze them under lest budget and schedule be adversely affected?

If you work for a defense contractor, does your firm give "special consideration" to government officials to get a contract, then pass this "cost of doing business" along to the taxpayers?

If you work for a car manufacturer, what does it do when one of its models has a dangerous mechanical defect? Does senior management recall the cars and fix them? Or do they weigh the cost of paying out death benefits if they didn't fix them, then choose to do nothing because it's cheaper to pay the death benefits?

These and many other exciting outrages are waiting for you on ***the first day*** ... and the many that follow. Make the best of them you can. Take the people you meet, the papers you are forced to sign and the situations you are thrown into with a grain of salt.

If you're going to let a little hypocrisy offend you, you might as well move to Oregon and raise organic vegetables with 50 year-old Hippies. You won't find any corporate officers forcing you to sign a Code of Ethics there. However, you will have to learn to enjoy dirt under your fingernails and old Jimi Hendrix records.

If this doesn't appeal to you ... if you enjoy modern amenities like indoor plumbing and cable television, force yourself to get through the first day!

PART TWO

THE PEOPLE INSIDE CORPORATIONS

INTRODUCTION

The People Inside

From the moment you walk through your first set of corporate doors, you will need to know how to deal with the various groups of people inside.

You'll quickly find that they already know how to deal with you. Most have circled the wagons and formed organizations called "departments". They've set up elaborate policies and procedures to make your life difficult, and theirs easy.

Learning how to turn the tables on them is one of the keys to surviving in a corporation.

CHAPTER IV

Accounting

The best thing that can be said about most accountants is that one day they will be replaced by computers.

This is just as well, because accountants tend to act like computers anyway. You know this is true if you've ever tried to convince an accountant that there is more than one way to do something. You might as well try to convince him that one and one do not equal two.

For those of us with a broader perspective, ***one*** Playboy centerfold and ***one*** Circus Fat Lady do not necessarily equal ***two.***

Accountants can't grasp this type of creative thinking, because to them, ***everything*** is numbers. Numbers always add, subtract, multiply and divide the same way. ***Always.*** There is no middle ground ... no grey matter between the black and white sides of an accountant's brain.

So, how do you deal with Accounting?

First of all, never talk down to accountants. This only encourages them to put anything with your name on it (i.e. your paycheck, invoice, etc.)

into a box for the new vocational school trainee to handle. Never ask them to do their job any quicker than they're doing it unless you have some incentive to offer them. Lunches in nice restaurants they can't afford often does the trick. Never utter a disparaging word about the supremacy of numbers. Numbers give an accountant's life meaning. They must never be questioned.

The best way to deal with accountants is to treat them with more respect than they deserve. Pump them up. Tell them how important they are to the company. Tell them you couldn't survive for one minute without them. Ask their advice on matters they have no business giving advice on. (But never ***take*** their advice!)

You may have to run home and take a shower afterwards, but at least you'll get your invoices paid and your paycheck on time.

I NEED SOME NUMBERS HERE —
SOMEBODY PLUG IN THURSTON

CHAPTER V

The Complaint Department

If you work in a corporation and want to register a complaint about some internal matter, don't waste your time looking for the Complaint Department.

It doesn't exist.

While corporations love to set up "customer service departments" to handle clients' and customers' problems, as far as the corporation is concerned, you have nothing to complain about. You have a job, right?

So count your lucky stars and get back to work before you get docked, you trouble-maker.

However, if you have been seriously wronged by a fellow employee or corporate policy ... if you have reached the point where your pride and honor are more important than your job, go ahead and complain. Make sure you have proof of your position, because corporations will support the person with the most authority when the evidence is not clear. If your evidence is unimpeachable, don't hold back!

For example, if your boss greets you each morning in front of the department with "Bring me my coffee, you sexy vixen bitch," this is still considered sexual discrimination in most states. You not only have the right to lodge a complaint with your Personnel Department, but the A.C.L.U. might even want to hear from you.

However, if you really want action in a corporation, take it to the ***top***. The bureaucrats around you base their corporate existence on finding new ways to keep things the way they are. They will not react to your complaint with anything but a polite nodding of the head unless they've been told to act by senior management.

Bear in mind that your job is on the line if you push any complaint too far, no matter how right you may be. Corporations do not care about the moral definitions of right and wrong. To them, ***making a profit is right***.

Not making it is ***wrong***.

As far as they're concerned, if profit is being made, there's nothing to complain about.

EMPLOYEES
COMPLAINT
DEPT.
WALK
RIGHT IN

CHAPTER VI

Facilities

The Facilities Department goes by a variety of different aliases ... Physical Plant Operations, Office Services, Office of the Building, etc., but they all have one thing in common:

The word ***"NO"***.

It doesn't matter what you're asking for, or how reasonable your request is, the answer is always ***"NO"***. Most Facilities people feel that everyone despises them because of the dirty, "service" jobs they do. One way they can maintain a sense of self-worth is to say ***"NO"***. This gives them a feeling of power over those who are constantly telling them what to do.

After all, Facilities is only one rung above Janitorial on the corporate ladder of respectability. Facilities people are not in the more "valuable" areas such as Sales (bringing money into the company), Production (making something for the company to sell), or Advertising (lying to the public about what Production makes so that Sales can brag about selling it). Facilities takes care of nitty-gritty problems no one else wants to deal with, like employees who lock the keys to their file cabinets ***IN*** their file cabinets, the misplaced personal mail of the Chairman of the Board and overflowing toilets.

If you've had to communicate with your corporation's Facilities department lately, you know that they are becoming more and more clever with their "***NO***'s". Common Facilities responses now range from "I can't do that without an approved requisition" to "It's not in the budget" to "We'll take care of that right away" (which means you'll be in a rest home by the time it's taken care of).

All of these comments mean the same thing:

NO.

There is a way of tricking Facilities personnel into doing what you want them to do, however.

First, if they tell you something can't be done, rest assured that it can. Before you can get Facilities to do anything, you need to have enough confidence to overcome Facilities' obligatory objections. Second, make them think you have enough clout to get them fired if they don't take care of your request.

If you hold a powerful position, you should have no trouble doing this. If you don't, here are some suggestions:

1. When asking for something, throw in a line like, "You know, I mentioned to the Chairman over lunch that I still haven't received that ***(insert your request here)*** I asked you for months ago, and it's keeping me from maximizing profit in my department."

2. Threaten to file a complaint with the appropriate authorities about "that stuff that looks like asbestos flaking all around the office" unless you get ***(insert your request here)*** .

3. Shower the entire Facilities department with candy, flowers, booze, nights on the town ... whatever it takes to get ***(insert your request here)*** . Any Facilities person worth their salt will go for a bribe.

The most important thing to remember about Facilities is that once you get around ***"NO"***, you can have virtually anything you want.

Just like many animals of the jungle, Facilities people are completely subservient once defeated. In fact, they'll be so eager to be your friend (they don't have many) that you can continue to get whatever you want from them as long as you work at your corporation.

You won't need a requisition, but you will need to know basic office commands like "fix!", "clean!" and "xerox!"

NO PROBLEM — JUST FILL OUT REQUISITION FORM #102B IN TRIPLICATE, HAVE IT APPROVED BY THREE SUPERVISORS, SEND A COPY TO LEGAL, THEN BRING THE ORIGINAL TO ME WITH A NOTE FROM YOUR MOTHER, A LARGE CASH GIFT AND A HUMMINGBIRD'S TONGUE.

CHAPTER VII

Human Resources
(a.k.a. Personnel)

Anyone who has ever come in contact with their corporation's Human Resources department knows that Hitler's Nazis are not hiding out in South America. They are alive and well and processing people in corporations all over the world.

To Human Resources departments, people are just that ... a "resource". No more important than the steel that goes into making a car, the polyester in a shirt, or the carcinogens in fast food. This is why many Personnel Departments have changed their name to Human Resources. Personnel sounded too much like "personal". Human Resources sounds more industrial.

Which is just the way corporations like it.

If you were to sit in on Human Resources meetings, you would hear employees being referred to in terms of numbers (i.e. salary figures, departmental employee "headcounts", benefit costs per employee, etc.), rarely as human beings whose feelings need to be taken into consideration.

Feelings just get in Human Resources' way. They are too busy processing people. Their methods are simple ... keeping salaries as low as possible, snuffing out any sign of unionism before it can breathe its first breath, and keeping voluminous files on employees so that there is always enough "in writing" to fire anyone without the hassle of a wrongful termination suit.

Naturally, this is not the image Human Resources departments display for public consumption. Part of their job is to portray Human Resources as a place where all employees have "an open door" to speak whatever's on their mind "in confidence", and receive "fair, equal treatment".

If you buy this, you probably donate heavily to TV evangelists.

The trick to dealing with Human Resources is to find ways to beat them at their own game.

Be the exception. Exceptions force bureaucrats to use their brains.

Human Resources departments hate exceptions, because exceptions cause changes in procedures. Changes mean more paperwork and take extra time.

So, if Human Resources insists on categorizing you, be a living, breathing human exception and complain.

For example, if they ever document anything about your performance, document them right back with the reason why they shouldn't be documenting you. Include several prominent labor attorneys on your cc: (carbon copy) list.

...AND A WARM WELCOME TO THE
CORPORATE FAMILY, WORKER-UNIT #B174XL-9!

This is very important! Human Resources lives in constant fear of wrongful termination suits. This type of litigation can be very costly for corporations.

As long as Human Resources has the slightest fear that you will sue if you're fired, you're probably in good shape. Encourage this fear!

Another fear Human Resources can't seem to get out of its system is what women and minorities will do if they are discriminated against. If you are female or belong to a minority group, you have a unique opportunity to take advantage of your corporation because of this.

Human Resources is under pressure to hire a certain percentage of you, and they don't think they can fire you unless you murder someone in front of at least 500 witnesses. They walk on eggshells around you lest an offhand remark insults you.

Encourage these feelings, as misguided as they may be. You've struggled long and hard against prejudice, and you finally have corporations where you want them ... at least psychologically.

This wasn't always the case. In the "good old days," the only corporate rainbow ran the gamut from lily white male to tan while male. Corporations relegated women to secretarial positions and minorities to menial labor. They hired as few as they liked, and fired anybody at will. Jokes about female body parts and minorities' work habits were abundant.

Times have changed ... or have they? Is the "Good Old Boys" system really dead?

Behind the cheery façade of "equal opportunity employer," corporations have become even more devious in their acts of discrimination.

When corporations total up the percentage of women and minority employees to make their hiring practices look good, they bolster the minority counts by throwing in ***white*** minorities. Take a look at your corporation's list of minority names. Squirreled away among the Garcias will be at least one Kozinski.

When was the last time you saw more than a few "tokens" in truly important executive positions? If your corporation does have minorities in these positions, how many lawsuits did it take to get them there?

Is your Chairman of the Board Black? Or Hispanic? Or Oriental? Or female?

If your answer to any of these questions is yes, you're in a minority yourself. If you are in this minority ... if you're lucky enough to work for a truly progressive corporation, cherish it.

But keep up the pressure.

If you don't, Human Resources' old ways will be revived. Just like the Nazis, Human Resources loves to smile in your face while planning your demise. They will tell you that "our employees are our most important asset," while behind your back they're sharpening up the bamboo shoots for a little "manicure".

SENATOR, I'D SURE LIKE TO INTRODUCE YOU TO OUR NEW MINORITY VICE-PRESIDENT — BUT RIGHT NOW HE'S PRETTY BUSY CLEANING THE URINALS...

CHAPTER VIII

Janitorial

How would you like to work all night long scrubbing toilets, emptying garbage cans and vacuuming miles of carpet ... only to wake up in the afternoon to find yourself accused of:

1) Not actually cleaning what you just spent eight hours cleaning...

OR...

2) Stealing 5 cents from somebody's desk...

OR...

3) Throwing away the ***ONE*** piece of paper that had the cure for cancer on it.

This is the life of a janitor.

Small wonder that most Americans think they're above this sort of work, and freely open their borders to any foreigner who will pick up mop and broom for minimum wage.

It is an unfortunate quirk of human nature that some people need to think they're better than others to feel good about themselves. These people have janitors to look down upon.

Everything in life has a bottom rung, and in a corporation the Janitorial Department is on it. After all, how many kids say they want to grow up to be janitors? How many employees ask for a transfer to Janitorial? How many janitors get invited to dinner parties at the Chairman's house?

If you are a janitor, you know how much confidence in yourself you need to be able to say that you clean up other peoples' garbage. You know that being a janitor feeds your family. You know that, while there may appear to be alternatives to this line of work, in reality there aren't many. It's unlikely that your application to become a 747 pilot is going to be accepted.

So, how do you make the best of what you do for a living? How can you bring the corporation down to the rung it's put you on and get it to respect you?

Here are some suggestions:

1. When you discover a top executive using his desk for various unorthodox sex acts, remember that minimum wage is much too low for an employee like you with this kind of knowledge and work expertise. Discuss your "finding" with the executive involved. You might even take a photograph for "insurance". Perhaps you are due for that raise and bonus after all!

2. When you are accused of doing stupid things you don't have the time, let alone the inclination to do ... actually start doing them. For example, if some snotty clerk tells you that you're shuffling the papers around on his desk when you really aren't, start! Then deny it

vehemently. Swear on your mother's grave (but cross your fingers behind your back). Ultimately, you will drive this moron who has nothing better to do crazy with suspicion that someone is spying on him.

3. When some egotistical, power-hungry executive tries to get you fired for not cleaning a speck of dust on his desk, make a point of talking about the time you "yanked a man's heart out" for talking behind your back ... just loud enough for the executive to hear. Modern day executives think they have all the power in the world until someone mentions the possibility of physical pain. Then they realize what the word "power" really means.

As for the rest of us, as much as we may be inclined towards the popular attitude that Janitorial is to be looked down upon, don't do it. The way corporations work, you, too, could one day be cleaning up other peoples' garbage.

I DIDN'T DOCK YOUR PAY LAST WEEK WHEN I NOTICED TWO PAPERCLIPS WERE MISSING FROM MY DESK, BUT THIS WEEK A ***PENCIL*** IS GONE!

CHAPTER IX

Office of the President

If you've ever wondered how King Louis XIV lived, take a peek inside your company's Office of the President.

Thousands of dollars worth of furniture, ashtrays that cost more than your annual salary, and a desk that hasn't seen a piece of paper since 1957 should be enough to make you wonder what the priorities of your company are.

If you need additional evidence that senior management is not working as hard as you, ask why your President is not in the office today.

If you can get one of his 42 secretaries to answer you truthfully, you'll find he's probably out at a "power" breakfast, playing tennis, "visiting" his mistress or doing any number of other things that prompted Karl Marx to start dabbling in economics.

For good or ill, the whole complexion of a corporation reflects the personal philosophy and lifestyle of its President. There are as many different types of Presidents as there are corporations to mirror them. However, a few general types can be found...

1. ***The Demagogue*** manages his company by allowing himself to be adored by his employees. He encourages such statements as "he truly cares about people" and "he's an all-around great guy just like you and me". This President can remember each and every employee's name as he walks down the hall in the morning. But this is where the nice guy image stops, because he also remembers everybody's name when he wants to engage in a little staff reduction. This type of President is just as cutthroat as all the rest. He just cloaks it differently. He knows that people will work harder when inspired than when berated. Hard working people help keep him and his company in the black. And so, just like a demagogic evangelist, he inspires.

2. ***The Meddler*** is the type who can't keep his hands out of every nook and cranny of the company. He thinks he knows how to do every job in the company better than his employees. They fear making decisions because they know they will be second-guessed. Gradually a paralysis sets in, and nothing happens without this President's approval, which generally means that nothing happens. Corporations run by this type of President usually don't last very long before they are bought out or go into "Chapter 11".

3. ***The Anarchist*** manages his company by not managing it. He is aloof, and prefers to let the company run by itself. This type of management usually gives rise to anarchy, with various department heads chewing each other up like wild dogs to win approval of a President who is oblivious. Often this detachment is a cover-up for a President who doesn't have the slightest

clue as to what he's doing. Makes you wonder how he ever became President, doesn't it?

4. The fourth type of President is the ***Bully***. He yells, screams, belittles, fires on the spot and never has a kind word for anybody. This management technique is called "rule by terror". Unfortunately, each act of terror must be followed by an even more barbarous one for this type of management to work. Otherwise, employees get used to being screamed at and learn to accept it. The only nice thing that can be said about this type of President is that the ulcers he usually gives himself are well deserved.

Of all the different types of Presidents, there is no one ideal type. Some are better than others. It's just the same with Presidents of corporations as it is with Presidents of the United States ... a crap shoot. You might get a President who negotiates peace treaties with our adversaries, or you might get one who brings the world to the brink of nuclear destruction.

Probably the worst thing the President of your corporation can do is lose some of the stockholders' money. Regardless of what ***they*** may think, that is ***not*** the end of the world.

WE'LL DISCUSS THAT REPORT WHEN I GET BACK FROM MY MEETING, HARRIS — AND I BETTER NOT HAVE TO REMIND YOU AGAIN ABOUT CORPORATE DRESS CODE!

CHAPTER X

Production

"Production comes first."

"Without production, there'd be nothing to sell."

"Production is the backbone of the corporation."

These and other narcissistic phrases are common expressions heard emanating from the Production Department. Production employees have to say good things about their jobs, because nobody else does.

Thus, Production employees try to make what they do seem as important as they possibly can. They walk with a swagger that suggests, "I can kick your butt just by ***thinking*** about it." They make fun of executives who can't fix their own cars. They form bowling leagues so they can wear jackets with their names stitched like a badge across the front.

The fact is, whether Production is manufacturing cars, drilling for oil or processing food, it's still doing the grunt work. The physical labor. The stuff no one else wants to touch.

Which would you rather do? Sweat all day long on a greasy assembly line, or sit behind a mahogany desk in your new Brooks Brothers suit debating the merits of the B.M.W. versus the Mercedes?

Because the economy can sustain only so many mahogany desks, Brooks Brothers suits and B.M.W.s, a lot of people wind up on an assembly line wearing jeans from K-Mart and driving a Chevy.

To most people, there's nothing wrong with wearing comfortable clothes and driving a car that gets good mileage. Most people, that is, except those who run corporations. They think that they alone know what the "best things in life" are. Because of this, they also think they know how to "manage" Production people.

Their standard corporate thinking holds that there is no reasoning with Production people, teaching them or in any other way treating them like human beings. That liberal feeling towards mankind many people had a brief fling with in college is to be avoided at all costs. Production people are to be treated like the animals they are. After all, how else can they be coerced into meeting unrealistic deadlines on shoestring budgets? How else can they be used to make the people above them look good?

This corporate method works ... but only so far. Sooner or later Production gets tired of being abused and rebels. Productivity suffers. Profits lag.

Even worse, corporate management's most feared demon ... the ***UNION*** ... begins to organize.

Corporate management's first reaction is to become angry and start firing people. Naturally, this only throws the rest of Production into constant fear of being fired, and productivity and profit suffer even more.

If corporations were smart, they would give Production incentives instead of demanding concessions. It's amazing how quickly productivity and profit return when people feel like they're working towards a goal other than just supporting the extravagant lifestyles of the people on top.

If you work in Production, don't expect to see this change overnight. It won't happen. So, don't take all of it so seriously that you give yourself ulcers. Have some fun with your oppressors!

If there is a particular senior executive who is giving you trouble, put his telephone number on the wall of a truck stop men's room. Order 100 sets of Ginsu knives and have them delivered to his office C.O.D. Every afternoon, make reservations in his name at a local "hourly" motel and leave his work number. Sooner or later, he'll get the embarrassing call! You'll get the last laugh, which is sometimes all that can be expected out of a corporation.

I'VE HAD IT WITH THE MISTAKES AROUND HERE. FIRE ANYBODY WHO CAN'T FIX HIS OWN CAR!

CHAPTER XI

Sales

"The most necessary evil in a corporation is the Sales Department."

How many times have you heard this statement?

You can look far and wide, but you won't find another group of people on earth who can conjure up a negative reaction like salespeople can. Mention the word "salesperson" to ***Quakers*** and even ***they*** become violent.

Why is this? After all, without salespeople to sell what a corporation produces, there is no revenue, no profit, and thus no corporation. Without salespeople, the entire capitalist system would quickly disintegrate. And the rest of us would be out of work.

So why do we hate salespeople so much?

Perhaps it's because of their stereotype. The common view of salespeople is that they exist only for the sale. When they close one, salespeople make money ... their only measure of self-worth.

Salespeople are seen as roaming aimlessly from corporation to corporation, hawking any and everything. The product is of little consequence to them. Selling computers may be a little more prestigious than selling industrial plumbing devices, but only a little.

Let's face it — selling is selling.

The multitude of personalities these salespeople appear to assume when dealing with customers makes Sybil look like a one-dimensional character. Best friend, father, mother, sister, brother, daughter, son, stud, whore ... you name it and they've tried it. Psychiatrists view these salespeople as steady meal tickets if they can get two or three of them on the couch.

Not a pretty picture, huh?

But is this stereotype real? Are all salespeople as disgusting as this? Would each and every one of them sell his mother into slavery if the opportunity to make a commission on the sale presented itself?

Or, are a few corrupt ones giving the rest of their colleagues a bad name?

Unfortunately, there are some salespeople who are unscrupulous and dishonest. They do everything that's been described in this chapter and more. These lowlifes deserve to have their Mercedes repossessed, then be forced to pull up to their country clubs in dilapidated Ramblers.

With these salespeople taking up valuable breathing space, the honest salespeople among us have to work twice as hard to be accepted as thinking, feeling human beings.

On the other hand, corporations are more than happy to see salespeople despised as much as they are. It keeps them vulnerable, and subject to easy manipulation.

Corporations love to play with salespeople like puppets.

Sometimes corporate management intimidates Sales by leaking word that they are not producing enough revenue, that the stockholders are "not happy", that "heads will roll". Salespeople immediately start running around like wounded animals. They know it is only one step from dinners at the finest restaurants to peddling door to door. If they don't continually satisfy their corporations' voracious appetite for profit, they'd better have a good pair of walking shoes.

But how do you, as an employee of your corporation, deal with salespeople?

If they work for your corporation, seek out the good ones and befriend them. They will be delighted to have a friend instead of a prospect, and they might even get you some good deals on something someday. Best of all, you won't have to listen to their sales pitches.

The bad ones, unfortunately, are convinced of their own omnipotence and are difficult to avoid. They demand everything they can get, and act as if everybody in the company works for them. It's difficult to discuss even the weather with these salespeople and not be reminded that the bottom line of the corporation is solely dependent upon their efforts.

So, don't discuss the weather ... or anything else with them. Just give them plenty of room for their egos. Eventually they'll collapse under their own weight.

For salespeople who come calling to sell your corporation something, treat the unscrupulous ones like dirt. They'll probably think you're complimenting them.

In a way, you are!

JUST THINK OF ME AS YOUR BROTHER, YOUR BEST FRIEND, DAD, MINISTER, BEER BUDDY, AND THE SON YOU NEVER HAD — NOT JUST SOME JERK TRYING TO CLOSE A SALE.

CHAPTER XII

Secretaries

Have you ever wondered why secretaries have an image problem?

It is largely due to the way they've been portrayed in movies and on TV. Beautiful but stupid. Fat and lazy. Underworked and overpaid ... these are just a few of the typical pictures that come to mind when one thinks of a secretary.

These are images that corporate executives are perfectly happy with. They hide the fact that secretaries do 99% of the work, but end up with 1% of the credit.

And 1% of the salary of those who claim the credit.

That's not to say that there isn't a small handful of incompetents who couldn't type a memo correctly if their lives depended on it. They ***do*** exist. This is unfortunate, because these few exceptions reinforce secretaries' image problem.

Corporations are delighted by this. They perpetuate the stereotype that secretaries are doomed to a life of answering someone else's phone. Secretaries are unpromotable, and even if they are promoted, they'll always carry the stigma of once having been a secretary. Once a secretary, always a secretary ... no matter what the new title.

If you're a secretary who wants to move up in the corporate world, you must reject this philosophy. It, like many other corporate conspiracies, is designed to keep you in your place and let others advance around you. If you are a woman, don't let corporations deflate your ambition when they promote men over you simply because you are a female secretary.

Fight back!

As soon as you can, shed your secretarial title. Lobby to have it changed to Assistant. Executive Assistant is even better. Take on as many non-secretarial projects as possible. Avoid getting coffee and doing personal errands for your boss. Go after any promotion you can.

Ultimately, you will have to jump to another company to truly shed the secretarial image of your past. Once you do, you'll find it's easier to move into other management positions from non-secretarial positions.

You must ***NEVER*** accept the second class citizenship corporations bestow upon secretaries. As long as you're a secretary, act as if your boss should be reporting to you, and not vice versa.

The way the corporate world revolves, one day he may be!

HER SHAMEFUL SECRET...

CHAPTER XIII

Security

It is often said that the misfits of the world who can't make it as real policemen become private security guards. The misfits of the world who can't even make it as private security guards go to work in corporate Security departments.

The heads of these departments are ex-police and would-be mercenaries who have opted for a safer way of life. Nabbing white collar criminals whose biggest crime is embezzling a few thousand dollars is a lot easier than fighting drug pushers in the streets or guerilla armies in Central American jungles. As long as they can control their sadistic urges, these department heads can be quite effective.

That effectiveness rarely extends to their employees, however. Most security guards are hired right off the street, slipped into ill-fitting uniforms and in many cases handed guns (to be used for ***lawful*** activity, for a change). These people usually fall into one of these three categories:

1. ***Cowboys***. Also known as "wannabees" (as in want-to-be a real cop), these gung-ho, violence-prone guards think they're the local police, F.B.I.,

C.I.A. and the SWAT TEAM all rolled into one. They walk like cops, talk like cops, and thirst for that big BUST to reaffirm their manhood. These guards think they've been hired to apply Green Beret tactics to the hallways of corporate America. Many times they do. It is not uncommon for a Cowboy's mind to snap over a simple little thing like an employee refusing to show his employee badge. Violent reflexes take over and the Cowboy fires a couple of "warning" rounds into the employee.

Because they're cops only in their own minds, Cowboys are no match for real policemen and real criminals. Fortunately for civilized society, Cowboys frequently end up in jail or the emergency room at an early age.

2. ***Cowards***. These security guards act even meaner and nastier than Cowboys and wanna-bees. They have to. They're hiding a deep fear of the world more overpowering than any act of violence. Cowards talk "big" about stopping criminals dead in their tracks, but if that entails snagging anyone tougher than a 90-year old paraplegic, they can be found in the nearest restroom with the dry heaves. While they're getting saddle sores waiting for what they consider ***"action"***, crimes are being perpetrated right under their noses that they don't even see. How many times has the biggest thief in the company walked out every night with a smile and a "howdy" for the security guard (who is more than delighted to be smiled and howdied at by ***ANYONE***), only to have it discovered later that he was concealing corporate assets in his unchecked briefcase?

How many times is a security guard accused of being the biggest thief in the company?

3. ***Fossils***. "Old" is not a strong enough word to describe Fossils. This type of security guard passed the age of 90 when he still had his eyesight, brags about the 10% hearing he still has in one ear and sticks a fork into an electrical outlet each morning to jumpstart his heart. Yet corporations still love to put a uniform on him and call him a "security" guard. They do this because the Fossil is cheap. They think that, because the Fossil is wearing a uniform, he will serve as a psychological deterrent to crime. Perhaps he is a deterrent to criminals in wheelchairs and hospital beds, but not much else. Still, the Fossil is loveable, and he'll let you get away with just about anything. Be sure to include him on your Christmas ham list.

When dealing with corporate security guards, remember that they will only do what they have been ordered to do. Conversely, they will not do anything they have not been ordered to do. Never offer them a creative solution to a problem. If it isn't in their orders, forget it.

This is not to say that Security is completely immune to manipulation.

Use a little flattery when you want something from Corporate Security, but don't be obvious. A statement like, "You look so strong and muscular in your crisp new uniform, I'll bet you could kill a criminal with your bare hands" is too blatant.

However, if you ask them to tell you cop stories, they'll be your friend and protector for life.

Telling cop stories reaffirms two important notions Corporate Security people carry around ... that they actually have some relationship with the real copworld (even if it is only telling stories they heard at a cop bar before they got kicked out) and that they have any authority at all.

So, become a one-person cop story audience. You'll have to stock up on No-Doz, but having a friend who wears a uniform and thinks he's a cop just might come in handy one day.

...AND THEN THEY TOLD ME I COULDN'T FRISK
NONE O' THEM FEMALE V.P.'S NO MORE!
HOW'M I EVER GONNA STOP WHITE COLLAR CRIME
WITHOUT THE "STRIP SEARCH"?

PART THREE

CORPORATE POLITICS

INTRODUCTION

Corporate Politics

Corporate politics are the driving force in a corporation.

Those with power use corporate politics to maintain it. Those without power use corporate politics to get it. Those with no hope of having power have no understanding of corporate politics.

If you really want to succeed in a corporation, you must ***PLAY THE GAME***. At first it will be distasteful. You'll be angry with your parents and teachers for raising you to believe that you can only succeed in life by doing things the ***RIGHT*** way ... that hard work and determination alone will pay off.

This *modus operandi* simply doesn't work. It never did.

Your parents and teachers were just passing this folklore on to you because they were afraid of what you'd become if they told you the way the world ***really*** works.

Surprise!

They should have told you the truth. You don't rise to the top of the corporate world by bringing milk and cookies in to your boss.

But politics aren't always as cutthroat as your worst fears. Often, politics can be made to work for your benefit with a minimum of bloodletting (yours or anybody else's).

Let's look at a simple, everyday example...

THE CORPORATION DOESN'T WANT YOUR
MILK AND COOKIES, HARRIS — THE CORPORATION
WANTS YOUR BLOOD AND GUTS!

CHAPTER XIV

People You Have to Suck Up To

Probably the most repulsive, yet effective application of corporate politics is "kissing the ass" of someone you detest in order to get ahead.

It will definitely make you sick. However, if you remember that it is only an act, you can view the whole thing with a kind of third person abandon.

So whose ass is worth kissing?

There are several obvious answers to this question ... the President of your corporation ... your boss ... senior executives. Basically, anyone you need to impress, or need something from.

One rear end that needs constant attention is that of your boss' private secretary. For some inexplicable reason, there is a small contingent of bosses' private secretaries who are:

1) Ignorant

2) Lazy

3) Forgetful

4) Revengeful

5) All of the above and more!

Although your boss may be the most intelligent, professional, and considerate person in the company, likely as not he has one gigantic blind spot when it comes to his secretary. No matter how horrible she may be, your boss thinks she can do no wrong. She has reached this exalted position because she controls all competition which might sway his opinion in the opposite direction. That control is exercised through...

Access.

And access gives her ***POWER***.

The power to grab your boss' ear at virtually any time and blame her own shortcomings on everybody else. The power to allow or deny you access to your boss at crucial times. The power to get you to do her work, making her look good in the process.

The power to make your life a living, breathing corporate hell!

There is no way you can fight this kind of power and win, so why not use a little corporate politics to keep it from being used against you?

Go ahead and kiss your boss' secretary's butt:

Laugh at her pointless jokes. Compliment her on her favorite dress ... the one that would get laughs at a Hawaiian luau. Agree with her that your pal in Research is a rotten son-of-a-bitch. Help her out when she has trouble scheduling a meeting with more than one person in it.

Administer the *coup de grâce* by giving her something she doesn't have to throw her weight around to get. It will shock and confuse her that someone has actually done something nice without being intimidated.

For example, let's say you control the company's parking assignments. One day, casually remark that you just happened to notice how far from the building she parks ... and what a long walk it is ... especially in the rain.

Then give her a new parking space ... right next to the building.

Like magic, you'll have constant access to your boss. He'll hear nothing but raves out of his secretary's mouth about you. You'll be her friend for life.

All you will have sacrificed is a little pride, some ethics, and a bit of your innocence. You will have played the game of corporate politics and won.

If this is as rough as corporate politics gets, corporations would be fairly tolerable places to spend the daylight hours.

Unfortunately for the squeamish, corporate politics are usually a lot more vicious...

MISS HIMMLER, I HOPE YOU WILL ACCEPT THIS RARE 94 CARAT DIAMOND AS A SPONTANEOUS EXPRESSION OF MY DEEP RESPECT FOR YOU ... BY THE WAY, DO YOU THINK I CAN GET IN TO SEE THE BOSS ***THIS*** MONTH?

CHAPTER XV

The Kind That Is Played For Keeps
(a.k.a. "Take No Hostages" Politics)

The people who play politics for keeps are true political beasts. They get what they want any way they can.

Corporate political animals are completely amoral ... and proud of it. They lie unabashedly, bad-mouth those who are a threat to them, and take every opportunity to make themselves look good at the expense of others. If these people didn't work in corporations, they'd be drug pushers, hired killers or United States Senators.

Corporate political animals are also ***VERY*** successful in business. If Johnny Appleseed and Al Capone were both working for a corporation today, who do you think would rise to the top? It wouldn't be the guy skipping around the country planting fruit trees.

Don't think for one minute that you can ignore corporate politics. Not "playing the game" will brand you someone who thinks he's better than those who do. A loner. An outsider. Someone who can't be trusted. Pretty soon you'll find your phone calls going unreturned, your memos ignored, your attempts to do your job frustrated at every turn.

The trick to playing the game is remembering that it is a game. As long as you do this, you can keep your mental stability. Those who are too deeply involved in corporate politics are so busy politicking that they've lost sight of how ridiculous it all is. You can easily fool them because they will take you seriously, no matter what you say or do.

Should you wish to play an advanced version of the game designed to cause great discomfort to the most vicious practitioners of corporate politics, start a rumor or two! Rumors are often the only weapon of those who can't marshall large departments, huge budgets or the support of the Board of Directors in their corporate battles.

So, spread the word that the arrogant Chief Financial Officer, who unjustly accuses his corporate rivals of stealing from the company, is about to be demoted to petty cash clerk and transferred to Nome, Alaska. Or that the shy little accountant whom everyone loves to abuse is about to be made head of the department. Or that the fat busybody, who uses her job as Employee Benefits Supervisor to poke into everybody's private affairs, is about to be featured in a supermarket tabloid cover story about suburban cannibalism.

Whether you're spreading rumors, or doing something even more vicious, enjoy playing the game. Your stress level will be less, and your chances of not keeling over from a heart attack at age 45 will increase markedly.

But don't ever think for one moment that you have cornered the market. The internal political games you play with your co-workers are extremely small potatoes compared to the politics corporations themselves play. Your corporation has been perfecting its political skills for a long time. It's ***very*** good at it.

After all, corporations are the most powerful entities in the world outside of armies. Anyone who believes that the government controls corporations and not vice versa hasn't been paying too much attention lately. Government, and this includes every office from the White House on down to Sanitation Engineer, seems to exist these days of, by and for corporations.

And why not?

Corporations fuel the money tanks of Washington, state capitols, city halls ... even small town councils. They do it through campaign contributions, gifts, honorariums for speeches and good, old fashioned bribes. Any politician or government official in a position to make a decision benefiting a corporation can profit. They don't even have to be elected any more. Career bureaucrats are easier to corrupt because they are further removed from the public's consciousness. All they have to do is put their hands out.

If their hands are full when they put them back in their pockets, these little "kindnesses" are remembered the next time these officials must pass judgement on some matter affecting the corporation.

For example, you're a corporation. You develop real estate. You want to put a subdivision in a national forest area. For some reason you can't understand, the birds, racoons and human environmentalists would rather have redwoods instead of condos in the forest. A grassroots coalition is formed to protest your plans.

Fortunately for free enterprise, you have supported the President ever since he was a money-grubbing little city councilman. A couple of phone calls later, you are directing the bulldozers and the environmentalists are wondering what hit them.

Like it or not, this is often how big time corporate politics is played. Unless you have as much money as your corporation, your voice will not be heard. However, as an employee, don't be afraid to criticize your corporation's actions when they offend your moral principles. Your corporation can't fire you for disagreeing. But be aware that a too altruistic stance can turn you into an outcast.

Unfortunately, people who are more concerned with human values than profit are always unpopular in a corporation. They don't get invited to lunch with the boss very often, but they do sleep well at night ... at least until they wake up one morning to find they've been demoted to Shipping Clerk.

Or fired.

HE'S COMPLETELY HONEST, HARDWORKING, SHARES CREDIT, NEVER BAD MOUTHS ANYONE — WHAT DO YOU THINK HE'S UP TO?

PART FOUR

UNLOCKING CORPORATE SECRETS

INTRODUCTION

Unlocking Corporate Secrets

There are many things your corporation doesn't want you to know. If you bother to ask, you will be told that they are confidential.

They are kept this way because if you and your fellow employees ever found out the truth about why corporations act the way they do, the resulting protest would make the French Revolution look like a grade school fist fight. Probably the most potent tool of corporations is secrecy.

The reason is simple...

Secrecy equals power.

The more you and your fellow employees are kept in the dark about what's really going on in your corporation, the more powerful your corporation becomes. The more powerful it is, the more power***less*** you are.

Some of the most fascinating corporate secrets include...

CHAPTER XVI

Who Actually Does The Work?

If you have to ask this question, you obviously don't.

If you know the answer, skip ahead to the next chapter.

To understand who actually does the work in a corporation, let's look at a simple hypothetical situation...

The President of a corporation wants to know how many cups of coffee are consumed each day by his employees. He is under the impression that uncontrolled coffee drinking by employees is a monumental financial drain on the corporation. In order to figure how much to start charging for each cup of coffee, he needs to know the consumption level. Since the President wouldn't have the faintest idea who in his company would know such a thing, he orders his secretary to find out.

His secretary doesn't have time to look for answers to stupid questions like this, what with trying to get her boss a good table for lunch and using his name to get herself a better table for dinner. She calls an executive she can manipulate ... the Vice President of Administration.

The Vice President of Administration wants to be anything but the Vice President of Administration. Having to come up with how many cups of coffee are consumed daily by employees is a further reminder that he is still the Vice President of Administration, and not the Chief Operating Officer or anything of real importance.

The reason he'll never become anything more important is because he is basically a no-talent kiss-ass. (A kiss-ass is a very valuable commodity in a corporation, even a no-talent one. A kiss-ass doesn't question his assignments, no matter how stupid they seem.) So the V.P. calls the flunky he hired to run around and get answers to the myriad of stupid questions he is asked every day ... the Director of Administration.

The Director of Administration's leading job qualification is his undying loyalty to the Vice President of Administration. Besides, the Director of Administration can't get a job on his own. The V.P. takes him everywhere he goes, because the V.P. needs someone to do the dirty work he is incapable of doing himself. The Director is, however, smart enough to call his Administrative Assistant for the answer.

Now, the Administrative Assistant has been with the company for a long time. Not only does she know how many cups of coffee are consumed daily by employees, but she can break them down by the cost per cup, the amount consumed this year versus last ... she even knows a practical way to reduce the amount of coffee employees are drinking, thus saving the company money (the

President's original goal, if anybody had taken the trouble to ask).

By now, you may have guessed that we've finally discovered who actually does the work in a corporation. The people on top will be the first to take credit for it, but the people on the bottom actually do it.

Back to our Administrative Assistant.

She is sitting on top of the answer the President is getting impatient for. If she gives her boss the answer, he and everyone else up the line will look good at her expense. At one time the Administrative Assistant would have done this. Way back then she truly believed that if she worked hard and supported her superiors, her abilities would be recognized and she would be treated fairly when raises and promotions were handed out.

Those naive, optimistic days are over, and the Administrative Assistant has reached her limit of incompetent and unappreciative bosses taking advantage of her.

The Administrative Assistant tells the Director of Administration that if he wants to know how many cups of coffee are consumed daily by employees, he should count them himself, as he might actually learn something about his job.

Fortunately, the Administrative Assistant has a job offer up her sleeve, so she can speak to her boss this way. No one without someplace else to go would buck the corporate chain of life with such comments.

But then, this is a hypothetical situation, and the President of the corporation just happens to be walking by when the Administrative Assistant tells her boss off. The President realizes that he has been shortsighted, that there was no need to populate his company with incompetent bozos like the Vice President and Director of Administration when he's had ***real*** talent like the Administrative Assistant working for him all along. He fires the V.P. and the Director on the spot, then gives the Administrative Assistant a major promotion and a big raise.

By the way, the only place you're ever going to see this ending is in the movies.

I'M NOT GOING TO WASTE MY VALUABLE TIME ON SILLY, POINTLESS NONSENSE, HARRIS — THAT'S YOUR JOB!

CHAPTER XVII

Incompetence

You may think that incompetence is merely a work performance problem that can be remedied by more training, more education or more attention paid to work.

Not so quick, Pilgrim!

It may surprise you to learn that incompetence is a talent corporations knowingly pay good money for. As hard as it is to believe, corporations frequently pass up experienced, competent people for their opposites. The reason is simple...

To ***SAVE MONEY!***

Let's say a corporation needs to fill a managerial position. An incompetent manager is cheaper to hire than a competent one. If a corporation can hire the incompetent manager with reasonable assurance his mistakes will not cost the company more than the difference between his salary and that of the competent one, it makes economic sense to hire the boob.

Always remember that ***economic*** sense is more important in a corporation than ***common*** sense.

For example:

INCOMPETENT MANAGER'S SALARY	$30,000
COST OF HIS MISTAKES	15,000
TOTAL COST	$45,000
COMPETENT MANAGER'S SALARY	($50,000)
SAVINGS GENERATED BY HIRING THE INCOMPETENT MANAGER	($5,000)

$5,000 may seem like a small amount to a billion dollar corporation. But $5,000 multiplied by hundreds or thousands of employees can be a savings that helps the bottom line tremendously.

What does it matter to a corporation that a few things get screwed up, as long as money is saved and profit increased?

One of the most frustrating things that can happen to an employee in a corporation is getting passed up for a promotion that goes to someone who is incompetent.

Usually, corporations have no idea whom to promote. For reasons that range from political to financial, good people get passed up all the time.

So what do you do if you are one of these good people? What do you do if you are passed over for someone who should really be under you so that you could fire him for being dead weight?

Your first inclination is probably to create a big scene, rant and rave about how many dedicated-but-unrewarded years you've sacrificed for the company, list the 1,001 reasons why the person who got the job is less qualified than you, threaten to quit, etc.

Resist this temptation!

At worst, it could get you fired. At best, it will give away your hand. The last thing you want known in a corporation is how you really feel about anything.

What you need to do in a situation like this is to remain calm. Don't let them know how angry you are. Don't let them know what a big mistake they've made. Pretend you understand why you didn't get the job. Pretend you are simply delighted with your new boss. Pretend you are giving him or her the benefit of your experience. You can always keep the most crucial information to yourself. Watching an incompetent boss fall on his or her ass is really quite amusing.

Above all, look for a new job.

Ten-to-one you'll find a better one, and better paying at that. Then you can walk out leaving them high and dry ... at least in your own mind. You won't, of course, because they'll just hire someone to replace you at a lower salary. Probably an incompetent! But the weeks, perhaps months of inexperienced bumbling the company will suffer at the hands of your new boss and your replacement should give you some satisfaction.

And while your corporation happily perpetuates its long-standing tradition of incompetence, you'll be someplace else where you'll be far better off.

FRANKLY, HARRIS, I'D PROMOTE YOU IN A MINUTE
IF ONLY YOU WERE A LITTLE LESS QUALIFIED.

CHAPTER XVIII

Cost Containment

Here's a little known secret for corporate survival and advancement:

If you want to climb up the corporate ladder faster than a relative of the Chairman of the Board, make cost containment your top priority.

In an age of corporate penny-pinching to protect profit at any price, cost containment has become the highest end to which any corporate employee can pledge allegiance.

Cost containment is like motherhood, apple pie and the American flag all rolled into one. You can't afford ***NOT*** to be for it. And, if you dare whisper anything against it, you might as well admit to being a communist, too.

So, jump on the bandwagon!

Come up with ingenious new ways to save the corporation money. Steal somebody else's old ways, change them just enough to avoid being called on it and propose them as your own. Form cost containment committees. Write memos to important executives telling them how much money you've saved in the last five minutes.

Criticize others for wasting precious corporate assets. Do anything you can think of to make it look like you actually care what happens to your corporation's money.

The ironic part of cost containment is that while you're busting your butt to save a couple of bucks, your corporation is squandering whatever you save like a high roller in Vegas, usually on an extravagant perk like mink covered chairs for top executives.

And, if you're not being totally honest, you probably won't admit that the money you save by cutting something in one place will be spent someplace else to make up for whatever you're cutting. For example, to save money and make yourself look good, you put cheaper hand towels in the restrooms. Now, they have to be cheaper for a reason. Usually, they are half as strong. People end up using twice as many to dry their hands, and the money saved by buying the cheaper towels is spent buying the additional ones.

Net effect: no real cost savings. Publicized effect: if you only show the initial savings, ***COST CONTAINMENT!***

But that's all part of the show, because cost containment is a shell game corporations use to convince their stockholders, Wall Street and ultimately themselves that they are being fiscally responsible.

In truth, the only kind of cost containment corporations really get excited about is ***staff reduction***. You can show corporate management a million dollars worth of savings by consolidating rental properties, reducing equipment expenditures, restricting telephone usage, etc. But you won't get their mouths really watering until you start talking about firing people.

What usually happens is this...

A corporation has had a bad quarter, which makes cost containment a hot topic. The Board of Directors puts pressure on the Chairman and the President, who put pressure on senior management, who put pressure on middle management, who put pressure on line management, who fire a few clerks and secretaries, thus reassuring everyone up the chain of command that the corporation is being fiscally responsible.

If corporations were truly fiscally responsible ... if they truly cared about cost containment, they'd cut in the only place where cuts make a difference:

AT THE TOP!

After all, the salary of one Senior Vice President is roughly equal to 11 Mail Runners' salaries combined. Corporations have a choice ... fire one Senior V.P. or 11 mail runners. If corporations were managed in a logical way, they'd dump a couple of excess Senior V.P.'s, save a hell of a lot more money and still get their mail on time.

You can easily guess what usually happens, and that explains why the mail in most corporations arrives late!

...BUT IF WE FIRE EVERYBODY WHO'S
UNDERWORKED AND OVERPAID,
WHERE'LL WE GET A NEW MANAGEMENT TEAM?

CHAPTER XIX

Corporate Lingo
(secret language)

After you've worked in a corporation for a while, you may find yourself speaking a strange new language. It is a language like no other, in which simple words and terms are purposely made more complicated than they really are. This way, the uninitiated think something important is actually being said.

It isn't. Corporate lingo is merely being spoken.

Some examples, and what they really mean:

CORPORATE LINGO	DEFINITION
"Open a dialog with him."	"Talk to him."
"Rectify operational deficiency."	"Do a better job."
"I'm going to do some xeroxing."	"I'm going to have some coffee, gossip with the girls and flirt with that new hunk of an attorney down the hall."
"What's our exposure on this?"	"How badly can we get screwed?"

"Initiate his termination processing phase."	"Fire him."
"C.Y.A." (cover your ass)	"Protect yourself any way you can, including blaming your mistakes on defenseless underlings."
"Our firm is downsizing to become more competitive."	"We're firing people left and right because our competition is flushing us down the toilet."
"There's no ego involved here."	"There's a world of ego involved here ... ***mine!***"
"Observe strict adherence to established procedures."	"Do what I say and don't question it no matter how stupid it sounds."
"What I'm telling you is totally off the record."	"This is good dirt. Spread it around. Just don't mention where you heard it."

Never pretend to understand corporate lingo when you really don't. Corporate lifers can detect this immediately, and will quickly turn on you with all the vehemence of a cornered rat.

There is a way to get back at these self-righteous bastards who think they've excluded you. Learn as much corporate lingo as you can. Then, when you've mastered it, make up corporate lingo words and phrases of your own! You can have hours of fun and enjoyment baffling others with things they're too embarrassed to admit they don't know.

Start small. Just a word or two.

For example, turn nouns and adjectives into verbs. Instead of "Say no to his proposal", try "***Negativize*** his proposal". Elongate words. Instead of "Include it in the report", try "Include it in the ***reportation***". Abbreviate. Instead of "I'll be at the Western Regional Office in Seattle-Tacoma", say "I'll be at the ***W.R.O.-SeaTac***".

When someone asks you what these things mean, give them that "what turnip truck did you just fall off of?" look. Then explain it to him as if you are scolding a child for soiling himself.

Soon you will be a master of corporate lingo, respected and feared by those who think they already are.

You must remember, however, to ***never*** take corporate lingo seriously. This country's mental institutions are filled with former corporate employees who became convinced that corporate lingo actually means something.

YOU CAN TELL THIS GUY HAS GOT A REAL BRIGHT FUTURE IN THIS CORPORATION — I HAVEN'T UNDERSTOOD A WORD HE'S SAID...

CHAPTER XX

Raises

There is nothing employees of a corporation like more than a raise.

There is nothing corporations like less than having to give one. This is because raises do only one thing to a corporation's profit margin ... ***shrink it.***

Many corporations seem to be psychic. Just when you finally work up the nerve to ask for a raise, they claim "diminished profits" and ask you and your fellow employees to take across-the-board salary cuts. If your corporation does this, start looking for a new job. You're going to need it sooner than you think.

To protect against the raid on the corporate treasury that would result from handing out raises when and where they're deserved, corporations use ***annual performance and salary reviews*** to keep wages as low as possible. For corporate management, this process is the only positive thing about raises.

If performance and salary reviews were judged as they should be, year after year they would win the Pulitzer prize for best fictional literature. Far from the objective job analyses they purport to be, these reviews are ingeniously designed to lump employees into strictly defined categories with preset increases.

This removes any chance of your being treated like an individual, and given an increase which is true compensation for your efforts.

Annual performance and salary reviews are managed in the best tradition of self-serving corporate bureaucracy. Before any raises are handed out, Human Resources determines the lowest annual increase percentage the corporation can get away with. Human Resources managers usually take an economic index such as the current rate of inflation, then pick a number which is lower. Thus, if inflation is running at 8% a year, they will recommend a company-wide increase of, say 6%.

The higher law to which all corporations pledge devotion (the much hallowed "profit motive") forbids any corporation from giving increases which exceed the current rate of inflation. Employees are given an increase designed to almost, but not quite, keep them at their current standard of living. Thus, they must keep working just to stay afloat. As long as all corporations follow this simple philosophy, there is less chance an employee of one corporation will have any financial incentive to jump ship and go to work for another. Further, no one is able to get far enough ahead of their bills to forsake the corporate way of life for independent living.

Back to the mechanics of how raises are determined.

The Human Resources manager presents his magical 6% increase to the Compensation Committee, a group of greedy senior executives who believe that every employee should feel lucky just to have a job. Compensation Committee members are pulling down six figures (at least), and have forgotten how difficult it is to survive on anything less. They cut the percentage down, from 6% to 5%.

The Compensation Committee then presents its percentage to the President and the Chairman of the board. The President and the Chairman couldn't care less about the percentage as long as it sounds low, because they must present it to the Board of Directors, who could care even less about the percentage, as long as it is low enough not to unduly reduce profit, and thus hurt the price of their stock.

So, in rapid succession, the President and the Chairman cut the percentage down from 5% to 4%, and the Board cuts it from 4% to 3%. By the time this entire process is over, a fairly insulting 6% increase has now become 3%, and gone from insulting to repugnant.

What do you do when your raise is less than it should be?

Standard corporate philosophy holds that you should swallow your pride, understand that your innate inadequacies are responsible for your low salary, and work harder. Then, maybe someday in the future you'll finally "earn" that raise you so selfishly covet.

This, of course, is ludicrous. Standard corporate philosophy is for people who need instructions above toilets. If you follow this misguided work ethic, you'll be lucky to walk away with social security when you're sixty-five.

Basically, you have two alternatives: leave the company or stay and fight.

If you choose to leave, be sure you have someplace to go. There is only one thing more difficult than being in a corporation, and that is getting back into one.

If you choose to fight, you must fight hard for what you deserve. No corporation is going to give you something it doesn't have to unless it is under significant pressure to do so.

So, threaten, cajole, write long, detailed memos ... anything you feel will work. Especially effective is that time-honored justification for a raise ... ***significantly increased responsibilities***. If your responsibilities have increased significantly, this means that you are doing the job you were hired to do, plus everyone else's in sight. If the corporation wants to keep you, then it has to cough up the bucks to pay you for subjecting yourself to this Chamber Of Horrors.

Be careful not to compare yourself to any other employee when demanding a raise. This is a trap corporations love to see people fall into, because they can then give a thousand and one reasons why the two employees are not comparable (i.e. length of employment, previous experience, job classification, etc.). It doesn't matter that a colleague of yours who dropped out of school, never had a job before in his life and has only worked for the corporation three days is making more than you. Your corporation will find a plausible reason why you can't compare yourself to him.

No matter how you fight, just remember the only one who ***CAN*** fight for you is ***YOU!***

You may be saying to yourself, "Yeah, but the corporation will never do anything special for me."

Don't believe it. Exceptions are made every day. But they're made for the noisy ones ... the ones who don't buy it when they're told that nothing can be done. The ones who aren't afraid to stand up for themselves.

If you aren't one of these people, ***become one!*** As quickly as you can. If you don't, corporations will run roughshod over you for the rest of your life.

HARRIS, IF IT WAS JUST UP TO ME, I'D GIVE YOU THAT RAISE IN A MINUTE — BUT I'M *ONLY* THE PRESIDENT OF THIS CORPORATION AND I MUST OBEY A HIGHER LAW — THE LAW OF THE *PROFIT!*

CHAPTER XXI

Sex, Love and Marriage

Once the ultimate taboo in the workplace, sex, love and marriage are now just as much a part of corporate life as coffee breaks.

This does not mean, of course, that you can carry on sexual encounters with the impunity of one sipping a cup of decaf. Because most people are embarrassed by sex, it is fodder for gossip. If too obvious, it can still ruin a career.

Thus, it is extremely important to differentiate between just having an affair, and truly looking for a husband or wife in a corporation.

Affairs

Many people (more than you think!) who work for corporations have affairs in the workplace. This is largely due to proximity. Since you spend more hours at work than at any other singular place, you meet more people there. Thus, it is more likely that a potential liaison is right down the hall.

SOME TIPS:

1. ***Be selective***. Arousal alone is not the first criteria for choosing a partner. Strange as it may seem, your sense of hearing should be consulted first. If the person to whom you are attracted has a big mouth, no matter how much the muscles of love may twitch, ***stay away!***

2. ***Be discreet***. After your affair begins, avoid the temptation to tell your friends at work. This is because not all of your friends at work are really your friends. Secrets have a way of ceasing to be secrets once you tell "the one and only person" you trust.

3. ***Be responsible***. In days gone by, the worst thing an affair at work could result in was your getting fired. Today, if you don't use good judgement and protection, an affair could result in your contracting a deadly sexually transmitted disease, like A.I.D.S. If you think you're going to be welcome in any corporation in that condition, think twice. Your corporation probably isn't going to sit still when its insurance premium skyrockets to pay for your treatment. Plus, dead people don't get paid. This is

good for the corporation's bottom line, but not so great for you.

4. ***Know when it's over***. Affairs that continue after they should have ended are about as pleasant as a bucket of raw sewage in your living room. The best time to break off an affair is just before either party gets too emotionally involved. Once this point is passed, you risk hearing comments like "There he is, the father of the baby I'm carrying, the bastard" as you walk down the hall with your boss. Things like this tend to interfere with career advancement.

Finding A Mate

If you ***are*** looking for Mr. or Ms. Right, your corporation can be a fertile field of opportunity. Depending upon your criteria, you can probably find just what you're looking for.

For example, if you are a woman who wants to marry a man with power and money, find any excuse you can to hang around the executive suite. If you are an executive, you should have no problem doing this. If you aren't, go there for a cup of coffee, to track down a lost memo, to use the "good" xerox machine, etc. Do not hang around places like Shipping. You won't meet many men there who drive B.M.W.s.

If you are a man looking for a beautiful, subservient wife, find any reason you can to summon women with a rank "lower" than yours into your office. For example, order as many reports as you can from the cute little 22-year old clerk in Central Files. If she starts bringing you files without being asked, you've as good as snagged her.

Do not show obvious romantic interest in people who are in positions with power over you unless you are fairly certain they will reciprocate. Even then, be advised that you are taking a serious risk, especially if it doesn't work out. People with power can and will use it for revenge when they are embarrassed by someone. The desire for sex, love or marriage can easily get you fired if not approached in the right way.

For example, calling the female Vice President of Business Affairs "babe" or attempting to touch her thighs could result in your contract being cancelled.

Likewise, assuming a seductive pose on your boss' desk without being asked is a good way to be sent back to the secretarial pool ... permanently.

Having an affair with the boss' secretary is another good way to end a career.

Although more sensitive because it is at work, there is a ***right*** way to approach the opposite sex. Make a point of "running into them" more often than usual, but not so much that it is obvious to others. Invite them to lunch or some social event away from work. Bring them a small gift that relates to some interest they have.

Leaving a condom and a suggestive note on their desk is ***not*** one of the right ways.

Whether it is sex, love, marriage or a combination thereof you are seeking, relations with the opposite sex can be fun and profitable in most corporations. Just don't let guilt get in your way. You may feel that you have no right to be thinking about romance on company time.

This is absurd!

If people in corporations concentrated more on romance than what they're ***REALLY*** doing to each other, the workplace might actually be an enjoyable place to spend eight hours a day.

...AND HERE ARE SOME FILES I FOUND IN THE TRASH THAT I THOUGHT YOU MIGHT LIKE

CHAPTER XXII

Stock, Mergers and Acquisitions

One of modern civilization's most pervasive myths is that a corporation's stock is worth more than the paper it's printed on.

Take a look at who actually owns a corporation's stock. The stockholders, corporations claim, are "average people", like the "guy next door", or "nice, little old white-haired grandmas" who've invested their life savings in "a few shares of stock".

This is about as close to the truth as jug wine is to Dom Pérignon.

Most shareholders may be the "guy next door" type, but the majority of stock is owned by the guys next door in Beverly Hills. Huge institutional investors have moved into the neighborhood too, as have foreign corporations. If you didn't master a foreign language in high school or college, you would be well-advised to pick one up now. It may be your native tongue sooner than you think.

Unfortunately, who owns the stock isn't necessarily the problem. The problem is how stock is manipulated to serve the narrow purposes of its

owners at the expense of a corporation's employees.

The most common forms of manipulation these days are mergers and acquisitions.

It doesn't take a brain surgeon to figure out why corporations love mergers and acquisitions so much. What other activities increase revenue, diminish competition, and give corporations an excuse to fire great numbers of employees ... all in one fell swoop.

Mergers and acquisitions give rise to the theory that corporations were invented by comedians, not businessmen. Many people see little difference between the two, but mergers and acquisitions really blur the line.

The problem with mergers and acquisitions is that they do not create anything except bigger, more monolithic corporations. They rarely create new jobs, products or services ... only rob the economy of money meaningfully spent and put it in the hands of a wealthy minority. This, by the way, is the only minority that people fight to get ***in***to.

You should be very concerned if you are working for a corporation that has become the target of a takeover attempt. There are several telltale signs. The most obvious is when your corporation starts lying more than usual.

"Our corporation is not a candidate for takeover" means the exact opposite.

Corporations that want to be taken over float rumors about how they've received offers of a buy-out, then make the above statement. This has the effect of artificially driving the stock price upward, thus making more money for the stockholders and top executives when the takeover actually materializes.

After a merger or acquisition has been announced, the lies get even bigger.

"No employees will lose their jobs."

When you hear this one, spread your resumé around town like wallpaper. Your corporation is just trying to keep the company intact so that it will not diminish in value while the deal is being consummated. When the acquisition is finalized, the new owner has usually paid too much. The corporation has been saddled with unmanageable debt, and must sell off assets and fire employees to pay for the acquisition.

"Our management team is here to stay."

Take a look at who occupies the executive suite after the acquisition. It isn't the old management "team" who just golden parachuted out. It isn't the former shareholders who are buying new Jaguars with the money they made from selling their stock.

It also isn't you. You're fighting the wolves to hold onto your job ... all because of the stock manipulations of people who couldn't care less whether you have a job or not.

But that's the way the corporation ... no matter who owns it ... wants things to stay. And so the real truth behind mergers and acquisitions emerges...

They only do one thing: replace one set of corporate owners with another.

Big deal!

TYPICAL STOCKHOLDER

PART FIVE

TAKING ADVANTAGE OF YOUR CORPORATION

INTRODUCTION

Taking Advantage of Your Corporation

Taking advantage of your corporation can be one of the biggest thrills of modern day life.

For people with any morals or ethics at all, it is difficult at first. They feel guilty.

Don't be dissuaded until you take a look around your corporation.

See how many people your corporation has hired to screw you ***(HINT: start with the Human Resources Department)***. Realize that your corporation has ways to take advantage of you that you haven't even dreamed of. Understand that when you are no longer useful to your corporation, you'll be gone. It won't matter that you didn't steal a few pens or take extra long lunches.

So, check your guilt at the door and ***take everything you can get!***

CHAPTER XXIII

Employee Theft

Should you include employee theft as part of your career path, you will have limitless opportunities.

You will also have a lot of competition, because virtually every corporate employee steals to one degree or another.

Most people engage in the most elementary form of employee theft ... taking stationery items home. A pen, a pencil, a few paper clips, some paper ... only the most dishonest hypocrite would deny engaging in this type of fundamental thievery. It's such a minor thing, most people don't even consider it theft.

Most people, that is, except for corporate management. Employee theft is a double whammy for them. The corporation loses money and an employee profits. To a corporation, that's a sin.

But as much as corporations would like to stop the theft of pens and pencils, it would take daily cavity searches of every employee to do it, and cost corporations more than they're losing. What really concerns corporate management are those ingenious employees among us who make off with the ***big bucks***.

The methods of stealing from a corporation are as many and varied as one's imagination will allow. Accountants cut checks made out to bogus companies they own. Managers approve timecards of fake employees who just happen to have their Uncle Rocco's home address. Senior executives sign deals on behalf of the corporation with companies they have a financial interest in.

These are the crimes corporations try to stop, because they cost a lot of money. While corporations pretend to be moralistic about all employee theft, it's the big ticket items they really care about. Their scale of morality tips towards indignation the bigger the amount of money involved.

Author's disclaimer: The author wishes to make it unmistakably clear that he does not condone, encourage or approve of any form of criminal behavior. But if you've already made up your mind that you're going to do it anyway and there is nothing the author can say that will stop you...

STEAL AS MUCH AS YOU CAN!

Don't fool around with amounts that will only pay for a camping trip to your nearest state park. Go for the gusto! Steal enough so that you can move to a country that doesn't have an extradition treaty with the United States, then live the rest of your life in unadulterated luxury.

Your chances of getting caught are the same if you are embezzling $500 or $5 million. Why risk jail over $500? And what if you get away with it? $5 million will get you into a greater quantity of fine restaurants than $500. And, if you do get caught, bear in mind that the people who steal $5 million usually get sent to nicer jails (i.e. minimum security "country club" prisons).

However, the best part of employee theft is not how much you get away with. The best part is that you're doing to your corporation what it usually does to its employees. But don't think you're doing something your corporation can't do ten times better.

Corporations "steal" every day by hiding income to avoid paying taxes, overcharging customers, not paying vendors, etc. Corporations can get away with this type of behavior because they are corporations. The local police aren't going to arrest your Chairman of the Board because his corporation doesn't pay its bills on time.

Doesn't it make you wish you could be a corporation? They have all the luck! This nasty business of being a real human being can be a pain in the ass.

G'NIGHT, MR. MOORE — PUTTIN' ON
A LITTLE WEIGHT, AREN'T YOU?

CHAPTER XXIV

Business Trips

At first, business travel may seem like a vacation because you're leaving town, but don't mislead yourself.

It is still work, so make your corporation pay ***THROUGH THE NOSE!***

Your corporation will try to control your travel expenses through elaborate policies and procedures designed to make sure you take the cheapest flights, stay at the cheapest hotels and eat at the cheapest restaurants. As far as it's concerned, you are not traveling for pleasure. You should be just as unhappy on your business trip as you are in the office. But, as they say...

Out of sight, out of mind!

A business trip is one of the last great opportunities to take your corporation for a ride, both literally and figuratively!

Here are a few helpful hints to make business travel work for ***YOU:***

1. Travel during work hours, not evenings and weekends. Your off-times belong to you, not the company. Traveling is just as much work as

what you do once you get to your destination. After all, you wouldn't be going there if it weren't for your job.

2. If you do a lot of flying, enroll in as many frequent flyer programs as you can. Keep all the mileage you earn for yourself. If a company auditor questions this, tell him you're the one risking your life in a steel tube 35,000 feet up in the air, not the company.

3. When making hotel reservations, impress your boss with how cost-conscious you are by booking your room at a Motel 6. When you arrive at your destination, "discover" that the Motel 6 is grossly overbooked, and the only available room in town is at the local Ritz-Carlton.

4. Include the people who approve, process and audit your travel expense reports on your ass-kissing A-list. When a questionable item comes up (i.e. a $500 bar tab you claim was for business purposes) you want these people on your side.

Whatever you do, be sure to spread your corporation's money around like water. Treat yourself to things you'd never waste your own money on. Order as much lobster as you can eat. Make long distance calls from your hotel room to as many friends and relatives as you can think of. Entertain business associates (and yourself!) with front row theatre seats.

If you do it right, you can travel like the Chairman of the Board, and never spend a cent of your own money!

THE BUSINESS TRIP

CHAPTER XXV

Taking Time Off

One of the best ways to take advantage of your corporation is to take as much time off as you can.

Corporations have statistics that stretch to the moon and back showing the adverse economic effect on the corporation of sick days, personal days, religious holidays, vacations, long lunches, etc.

What about the adverse effect on an employee of having to work a full work-week? Especially the employee who watches her boss come in at ten, take a two-hour lunch at noon and then leave at four.

You have no obligation to feel guilty about the little extra time you squeeze out of your corporation until the guys on top stop doing it too. Rest assured they're taking a lot more time off than you.

Doctor's Appointments & Calling In Sick

One of the best ways in the world to take time off is to use a medical excuse.

Alleged "doctor's appointments" are rarely, if ever questioned. Most bosses won't ask why you are going to the doctor. If they do, have an excuse ready. Ladies always have the never-challenged "women's problems".

Bogus doctor's appointments are flexible. You can "schedule" them early in the day and come in late. You can "schedule" them in the middle of the day and extend your lunch hour. Or, you can "schedule" them in the afternoon and leave early.

If you feel you are being watched, make a couple of obvious (but fake) calls confirming your appointment, then make a big scene of getting the insurance form to take with you.

When you are desperate for time off and all else fails, get sick!

Calling in sick is an art form all its own. Before you do anything, pretend you are in great pain. Then, muster up your most gravelly, hoarse, weary voice and call your boss. Be sure to mention how you were up all night with the "stomach flu". Offer to be a martyr and drag your wretched, aching body in if he needs you. No matter how much your boss may think you're faking it, he has no way of really knowing. Plus, your boss doesn't want you to come in and give whatever you have to other employees. It's not that he really cares about their health ... he can't afford to lose even more productivity. If he's extra gullible, he might even send you a card.

There are certain precautions to be taken when calling in sick. Do not go anywhere near your workplace, especially to restaurants where you might be seen. Don't spend too much time outside, as a suntan is hard to explain when you were supposed to be home vomiting up your chicken soup. Don't tell anyone at work that you're not really sick ... ***EVER!***

As far as everyone is concerned, you're one call away from the emergency room.

THIS IS THE C.I.A. HARRIS CAN'T MAKE IT IN TODAY. HE'S BEEN ABDUCTED BY TERRORISTS AND TAKEN TO IRAN — BUT HE'LL PROBABLY BE IN TOMORROW...

The Lunch Hour

Executives take ones that last three hours, then write them off as "business". Factory workers have a lunch ***half***-hour — barely enough time to scarf down a cold sandwich. Office workers rarely get to eat. Their "lunch" time is spent squeezing in personal things they can't do during normal work hours (e.g. standing in line at the bank, renewing driver's licenses, last-minute shopping, etc.).

No matter what you do on it, no hour of the day is more eagerly awaited than the lunch hour ... except for quitting time. Corporations don't particularly like lunch hours because they represent time away from work. They only tolerate them because employees are less productive on empty stomachs. Plus, the nasty old courts come down pretty hard on corporations that don't give their employees the breaks they are entitled to by law.

Unfortunately, many people take their lunch hours for granted. Do ***NOT*** do this. Here are a few tips to make yours more enjoyable:

1. ***NEVER*** eat at your desk. You will only feel like doing work, and people will assume you ***are*** still working because you haven't left your desk. You might as well hang a sign around your neck which reads: "Please bother me," because they will.

2. Do not eat lunch with people whose only topic of conversation is what goes on at work. You might as well eat at your desk.

3. ***ALWAYS*** look around in a restaurant to see who is seated near you before gossiping. Jobs have been lost due to careless remarks overheard by the wrong person.

Vacations & Holidays

People who don't take off holidays and let years go by without taking vacations are masochists.

If you think your corporation is going to promote you faster or give you a bigger raise because you sacrifice legitimate time off "for the good of the company", you are in serious need of psychiatric care. Your corporation is getting quite a bargain. It pays you a straight salary, yet you work holidays and weekends. Do you have any naive brothers and sisters back home who need jobs?

Rest assured the corporation will find many ingenious ways to take advantage of you over the years — don't make this any easier for them. If you continually volunteer your own time, soon the corporation will come to expect it of you. Then, the day you tell your boss, "This year, I won't be in on Christmas Day," he'll probably fire you for insubordination.

For those of you who ***do*** take your holidays and vacations (hopefully ***MOST*** of you), don't ever forget that these off-times are to be fully exploited. You've earned them, so enjoy them.

Do ***NOT*** leave telephone numbers where you can be reached.

Plan vacations around holidays so as to minimize actual vacation days you must use up (i.e. if the Fourth of July lands on a Monday and you take it off, as well as Tuesday through Friday as vacation days, you've only used four actual vacation days, but get away from work for a whole week!).

Leave town.

But, above all, whether it's sick time, a lunch hour or your vacation, your off-times are yours. You've earned them.

If that isn't enough to convince you to take them, bear in mind that they cost your corporation money.

Bon voyage!

PART SIX

GETTING OUT OF A CORPORATION

INTRODUCTION

Getting Out of a Corporation

There are basically two ways to get out of a corporation ... the kind where you make the decision and the kind where somebody else does.

It is recommended that, whenever possible, ***YOU*** make the decision. When you make the decision, you have many options. When somebody else does, you have only one.

Getting out of your corporation can be a rewarding experience, if ***YOU*** do it by...

CHAPTER XXVI

Quitting

Quitting is when you ***choose*** to leave.

There are many reasons for quitting a job. Some people quit because they've found a new job. Some people quit to retire. Some people quit to prevent nervous breakdowns. Some people even quit their jobs out of principle, although this option is mostly limited to lottery winners.

The most important thing to remember about quitting is that no matter why you think you're doing it, you're really doing it for yourself. If you aren't, then you shouldn't be quitting.

Only a moron would quit his job because the person in the next cubicle smoked, or picked his nose in a loud and annoying way, or ate herring all day long at his desk. These may be reasons for attempted murder, but not for quitting a job.

One of the most exhilarating feelings you can experience is quitting a bad job. Especially when you have a better one to go to.

When you actually get to do this, savor the moment. It doesn't come often.

But remember that no matter how much you think you're hurting your corporation by leaving, you're not. As we learned earlier, the minor disruption your departure causes is tolerated because you can now be replaced by a lower paid employee.

WELL, I'M SORRY YOU'RE QUITTING, LOOMIS;
I'D BEEN LOOKING FORWARD TO FIRING YOU.

Some hints to make the quitting easier on ***YOU:***

1. To be polite, give at least an hour's notice. Some may think this is too short, that "standard business procedure" dictates two weeks. Remember that "standard business procedure" was not devised by employees who quit, but rather by corporations that need time to replace them. You can give more than an hour's notice if you feel so moved, but how much notice would your corporation give you if it fired you? Just enough time to clean out your desk, if you're lucky.

2. If Human Resources asks to conduct an exit interview, gladly participate. They always ask for your candid comments on "how to make the company a better place to work". Since you're leaving, theoretically you should have no qualms about being totally honest. Be so honest it makes their toenails sweat! Criticize everything about the company you hate. Get your enemies in trouble by pointing out who's on the take and who's incompetent. Insinuate that someone is tasting "delicacies" only the Chairman's wife can "cook up". Have some fun! You'll never have to deal with these people again. End your exit interview by demanding confidentiality ... or you'll sue!

3. Take souvenirs. Stationery items are nice, as are pictures, plants, other "gifts" you feel the corporation owes you ... basically whatever you can get to your house without the aid of a moving van.

If you haven't guessed by now, quitting is an activity that can be as much fun as you choose to make it. Enjoy it, because it sure beats...

CHAPTER XXVII

Getting Fired

What do you do if that most dreaded of all corporate evils occurs and ***you get fired?***

First of all, raise hell! Don't pass up this opportunity to tell your boss everything you've always wanted to tell him, but were afraid to because you thought he'd fire you. Guess what? He just did. Now you can unload. Be particularly nasty, because that's what people doing the firing fear most. In fact, many of them have sleepless nights worrying about what the person being fired is going to say when the ax falls. If you go quietly, you only make it easy for them.

Second, do some real soul searching. Reach way down into your subconsciousness and ask yourself whether or not you are the cause of your predicament. No matter what you come up with...

SUE THE BASTARDS REGARDLESS!

You may not have a case, but this doesn't really matter. Your suit will tie up the corporation's lawyers for years. It will cost time, money and much inconvenience. Best of all, your corporation will probably end up settling out of court with you just to get you off its back. Isn't it ironic that one of the few ways to get good money out of a corporation is to be fired?

It's even better if you can claim some sort of discrimination. Discrimination suits terrify wimpy little M.B.A.'s who think that firing people is just a corporate game with no penalties.

Unfortunately, the quality of justice you receive is directly dependent upon the size of your wallet. If you are fairly well off, suing should be no problem. If you aren't, don't let that stop you. There are legal aid societies, do-it-yourself legal books, the A.C.L.U., the N.A.A.C.P. and a host of other places to go for help if you were wronged. Don't let a lack of money stop you from exercising your rights.

Your corporation is betting it will. ***Surprise it.***

But before you go through all this torture, try to avoid getting fired in the first place. The best advice about getting fired is still, if you can at all help it...

DON'T!

No matter what you may have heard, getting fired still carries a stigma. The only place where this isn't true is in Hollywood, where getting fired is like getting a promotion. Showbiz people who haven't been fired by every studio in town at least once are considered amateurs. But, most likely, if you are reading this book you are not a Hollywood movie mogul or a Prime Time TV star.

You probably work a "regular job". You put in 40 or more grueling hours a week. You need every cent you make. Getting fired would be the worst thing that could happen to you and your family.

Preventing it is all-important.

The best way to avoid being fired is to intimidate your corporation. All corporations are terrified of wrongful termination suits. Thanks to our judicial system, many fired employees with the weakest and most ridiculous of cases are actually winning them. Because of this, corporations do headstands to ensure that the transgressions of any employee they want to fire are documented to the hilt. These days, if you look at your boss the wrong way, this is "written up" and put in your personnel file. Later, your corporation can say you were warned, given time to fix whatever was wrong with your performance, but that you didn't improve.

It's easy to get around this Orwellian bureaucracy. If your corporation blames some imperfection of nature on you, blame it on your corporation's policies and procedures ... or lack of them. If it claims you did something wrong, claim you did it with the full knowledge and approval of your supervisor.

Don't ever let a criticism go unchallenged. If they really want to fire you, they'll find a way. But your preventive counterattack will slow them down.

Most important of all, don't allow yourself to be a victim. When a corporation fires you, it is not just carrying out a personnel procedure. It is attacking you in the most personal sense. It is taking away your income, and thus threatening the survival of you and your family.

The least you can do is threaten your corporation a little bit in return!

CONGRATULATIONS, HARRIS —
I HEREBY PROMOTE YOU TO VICE-PRESIDENT
AND AUTHORIZE YOU TO FIRE MULDOON

CHAPTER XXVIII

Retiring

If you're nearing retirement, presumably by now you've figured out how to survive working in a corporation. If you haven't, there's nothing this book can do for you.

However, if your retirement seems as far in the future as false teeth and rubber underwear, a word to the wise:

PREPARE NOW!

The old jokes about a handshake and a gold-plated watch are often true. Unless you've been guaranteed by competent geologists that your back porch is sitting on a motherlode of gold, you'd better start socking away money ***now***. There are a variety of ways to do this, from pension plans to I.R.A.s. It doesn't matter how you do it, just do it. Once you're out there without a corporation to pay for the little luxuries of life like food and clothing, your only source of income will be social security and whatever you've saved.

If you need any more inspiration than this to act now, take a tour of your friendly neighborhood retirement home. Many of them take in old people for the price of their social security checks. This is hardly enough to pay for quality care. And, be sure to take a can of insect repellent so you can clear a path through the army of roaches.

Most importantly, do not expect anything out of your corporation. It is more than happy to see you retire, because yours will be one less paycheck they'll have to write. They will even grumble about having to put out a few measly bucks to give you a retirement party.

Many corporations offer early retirement packages to induce employees to leave work before retirement age. Like everything else a corporation does, early retirement is portrayed as good for employees when in fact it benefits the corporation more. The corporation profits in the long run by, again, not having to cut a paycheck. Seek expert financial and legal advice before accepting an early retirement package.

Many corporations also have a way of making you retire against your will. This is a clever form of firing called mandatory retirement. It's your corporation's way of saying that, because you are old, you can no longer do your job.

This may be true if you are a tightrope walker.

And, a 69-year-old saleswoman may not be able to chase after customers as quickly as her 18-year-old counterpart. However, the 69-year-old has a lot more experience dealing with customers, knows a lot more about her product, and even has a few more tricks up her sleeve.

She also makes more than the 18-year-old, which is why the corporation wants her out. So, never be fooled by your corporation. Mandatory retirement is a concept born of economics, and nothing else.

And economics is what you should consider when you think about retiring.

Your economics.

WE'RE ALL HERE TO HONOR FRANK TUCKER, WHO'S RETIRING AFTER 40 FAITHFUL YEARS WITH THE COMPANY. SO, FRANK, WE SAY THANKS, GOOD LUCK, AND HERE'S A COPY OF THE COMPANY CALENDAR! NOW EVERYBODY GRAB A CUP OF PUNCH AND THEN WE'LL DRAW STRAWS FOR HIS OFFICE.

CONCLUSION

Between the covers of this book, we've explored how to survive working in a corporation.

We've looked at what corporations say they do, and what they actually do.

We've discussed ways to put corporations to work for you, rather than the other way around.

And we certainly haven't shied away from their shortcomings!

But is the corporation solely to blame for all the ills of society? Are we right to hold it totally responsible for heaping untold suffering upon mankind?

Perhaps not, but something is definitely wrong with a structure that:

1. Emphasizes profit, no matter the human cost.
2. Rewards following orders at the expense of individual initiative.
3. Allows those on the top to maintain power by repressing those below.

4. Maintains a veil of secrecy about its actions, and punishes its critics.

Sounds a little like a dictatorship, doesn't it?

Uh oh! Heresy!

Many of you are probably trotting out that old standard line designed to give us all warm cuddlies:

"Our system may have its faults, but compared to the alternatives, it's still the best."

The best as compared to what? Is working in a corporation really better than living in a dictatorship?

In a dictatorship, you can't criticize your leaders without fear of repercussions. Ever try criticizing the President of your corporation and still expect a future there? In a dictatorship, most people don't make much money and can barely get ahead, while those on top prosper. Have you looked at how far your paycheck takes you these days? Ever compare it to a paycheck of someone in senior management? In a dictatorship, everybody works long hours at a job they hate, with little hope of ever doing anything different.

Are you really doing what you want to do with your life?

The purpose of this book has not been to simply defame corporations or suggest that any other alternative would be a suitable replacement. But something better ***can*** be achieved ... ***must*** be achieved if corporations are to advance beyond the robber baron mentality that permeates so many of them.

Rest assured that little or no improvement will come from the shareholders or management. They have too much invested in the way things are to appreciate the way things could be.

The change must come from ***you***.

So, take the secrets about corporate survival you've learned from this book and ***go kick some corporate butt!***

WELL, NOW ***I'M*** WAITING!

ABOUT THE AUTHOR

Scott Choate makes his home in Los Angeles, California, where he has worked for several major corporations to support his writing habit.

Mr. Choate hopes you will urge all of your friends to buy this book so that the only corporations he will ever have to work for again are the many fine book publishers across the land!

—BEST SELLERS—

GETTING EVEN WITH THE ANSWERING MACHINE................$3.95

By John Carfi & Cliff Carle (ISBN 0-918259-01-0)

Have fun when you reach your friends' machines! Practical jokes, gags, funny and clever quips. By the authors of the bestselling No Hang-Ups book.

HOW TO GET EVEN WITH YOUR EX.........$3.95

By Marsha Posner Williams & Mike Price (ISBN 0-918259-09-6)

1986 Emmy Award winning producer and syndicated columnist teamed up to solve the age-old problem of all those frustrating EXes (not just husband and wife) in a therapeutically deliciously funny way.

HOW TO SUCCEED IN SINGLES' BARS (For MEN Only) $3.95

By Cathi Chamberlain (ISBN 0-918259-04-5)

A former Playboy Bunny's step-by-step guide to meeting that "special someone". Find out what single women are looking for in men!

TOTALLY OUTRAGEOUS BUMPER-SNICKERS............................$2.95

By Eager Allen Poe, Mark Not-Twain, Kent Clark (ISBN 0-918259-13-4)

A collection of the nation's funniest bumper stickers, with a coupon for ordering a 'create your own' kit.

—ACCESSORIES—

CREATE YOUR OWN BUMPER STICKER KIT $2.95

(ISBN 0-918259-19-3)

Any bumpersticker or sign can be yours with this easy-fun-to-do kit.

THE "MAGIC BOOKMARK" BOOK COVER (Vinyl — 2 Sizes)

Revolutionary new book cover!

SMALL.. $1.95

(Mass Paperback) (ISBN 0-918259-10-X)

LARGE.. $2.25

(Oversize Trade Paperback) (ISBN 0-918259-11-8)

You will never lose your place or have to dog-ear a page again! As you turn each page, the bookmark automatically falls onto the next page. Whenever you close the book your place is automatically marked — even if the book closes accidentally. Great for reading in bed, at the beach, on airplanes or anywhere on-the-go. Two sizes, 4 1/4" x 7" (mass paperback) and 5 1/2" x 8 1/2" (oversize trade paperback).

—CASSETTES—

NO HANG-UPS TAPES...............................$4.98
(Pre-recorded outgoing a.m. messages w/all digitally mastered lazer CD effects)

VOLUME V: CELEBRITY IMPERSONATIONS

VOLUME VI: FOR SPORTS FANS

—BEST SELLERS—

Volume I: GENERAL MESSAGES
Female Voice: ISBN 0-918259-02-9
Male Voice: ISBN 0-918259-14-2
(20 of the best from the bestselling No Hang-Ups book)

Volume II: BUSINESS MESSAGES
Female Voice: ISBN 0-918259-06-1
Male Voice: ISBN 0-918259-15-0
(For all business answering machines — enhance customer relations in your absence)

Volume III: 'R' RATED
Female Voice: ISBN 0-918259-07-X
Male Voice: ISBN 0-918259-16-9
(Have your phone answered by some of the nation's top Adult Movie Stars, including John Holmes! These suggestive-but-soft-core messages will add a little "spice" to your machine!)

Volume IV: Sound Effects Only ISBN 0-918259-17-7
(Provides exciting and funny background effects — allows you to use your own voice. Suggested scripts included)